RAINBOW WINGS

A Young Girl's Journey to Heaven and Back

TAPPE HOPSON

Rainbow Wings: A Young Girl's
Journey to Heaven and Back

Copyright © 2025 by Tappe Hopson

All rights reserved. No part of this book may be reproduced, stored, or transmitted without written permission from the author. No portion of this work may be copied, stored in a retrieval system, or shared in any form—electronic, mechanical, photocopying, recording, or otherwise—without prior authorization, except in brief quotations for reviews or articles.

This is a work of non-fiction. The events and reflections shared are true to the author's experience and memory. Names and identifying details have been changed where necessary to protect the privacy of individuals. The author has made every effort to portray events truthfully while honoring the dignity of those involved.

Printed in the United States of America
ISBN (eBook): 979-8-9986170-0-3
ISBN (Print): 979-8-9986170-1-0
First Edition: August 2025

Published by **Tappe Hopson Publications**

For permissions, inquiries, and additional resources, visit:
https://www.tappe-hopson-publications.net

Scripture quotations taken from
The Holy Bible, New International Version® (NIV®)
Copyright © 1973, 1978, 1984, 2011 by Biblica, Inc.™
Used by permission of Zondervan. All rights reserved worldwide.
www.zondervan.com

"The NIV" and "New International Version" are trademarks registered in the United States Patent and Trademark Office by Biblica, Inc.™

Dedication

To my beloved parents,
Marie Pirtle Hopson and Robert A. Hopson Sr.,
who have already earned their *Rainbow Wings*.

Your love, wisdom, and strength continue to guide me,
even beyond the veil of this world.

May your journey be filled with **heavenly light**,
and may your spirits **soar in eternal peace and joy**.

Table of Contents

Introduction 1

Chapter 1: A Hopeful Journey 6

Chapter 2: A New Journey.. 15

Chapter 3: A Journey of Loneliness 23

Chapter 4: A Journey of Strength... 39

Chapter 5: Navigating the Medical Journey 49

Chapter 6: The Surgical Journey..57

Chapter 7: An Unexpected Journey: A Glimpse Beyond................ 67

Chapter 8: Trusting the Journey: Why I Believe in My Daughter's Heavenly Experience 79

Chapter 9: Reflections of a Heavenly Journey................................ 88

Chapter 10: Embracing the Next Chapter...................................... 100

Afterword: Trusting the Journey... 111

Introduction

"For I know the plans I have for you, declares the Lord, plans to prosper you and not to harm you, plans to give you hope and a future."
– Jeremiah 29:11

There were times when I questioned the path before me. Was this truly God's plan? As I walked through uncertainty, this verse reminded me that God sees the bigger picture. His plans may not always align with mine, but they are always good—always purposeful.

On April 14, 2015, I had a dream so vivid, so staggering, that it forever altered the way I saw life and faith. My three-year-old daughter, Amariah, was at the heart of it. The vision came during an otherwise routine drive—tranquil and sunlit—along Interstate 64 from Norfolk to Virginia Beach.

Then, I saw it.

A radiant figure bathed in light appeared before me, motioning toward an unexpected exit—one to the left. Confusion flickered through my thoughts; exits are always on the right. But something beyond logic urged me forward. The atmosphere shifted. I was no longer simply driving—I had been transported into a realm of indescribable beauty. Golden light stretched before me. Peace wrapped around me like a warm embrace.

Yet, the moment was fleeting. As I steered toward the left exit, the celestial serenity dissolved, replaced by chaos. The peaceful drive turned to devastation—wreckage littered the road, shards of metal and glass glinting under the unforgiving sun. Sirens screamed in the distance. My breath caught when I saw the remains of a yellow school bus marked "Virginia Beach Public Schools." My daughters were on a field trip that day.

Panic clawed at my chest as I searched for them. Then I spotted Michaela, my eldest. She was unharmed, though streaked with a mix of dirt and blood and wearing lilac surgical gloves. Despite her own injuries, she was helping the wounded—young children lined up along the road, their faces pale with pain, their small bodies marred with wounds both deep and cruel.

But there was no sign of Amariah.

I turned, desperate, scanning every face. Then, something strange happened. The police officers and medics stopped working. Their gazes fixed on me. Murmurs rippled through the crowd: *I'm sorry for your loss.*

Loss?

A medic stepped forward, placing a shimmering, iridescent box in my hands. It was beautiful, shifting colors as it caught the light. But dread settled deep in my bones. What was inside?

I opened it.

Inside, curled in a fetal position, lay my sweet Amariah. She was dressed in flowing white, peaceful as an angel, untouched by the chaos around her. Tears spilled down my face as a single thought consumed me: *No. My baby is not dead.*

A fierce determination surged within. I cried out to God: *Help me.*

And then—I was elsewhere.

The golden path stretched before me again, guiding me to a clay-brown home. Stepping inside, I felt an undeniable presence. Time folded in on itself. I stood in the home of Jairus, watching Jesus approach his daughter. His eyes were full of compassion, his voice steady as he spoke the words I knew from Luke 8:51: *Damsel, arise.* The girl opened her eyes and sat up—alive once more.

A sob caught in my throat as Jesus turned toward me, warmth radiating from his presence. "I have given you the authority to do the same, Tappe," he said. "Tell your daughter to rise."

I trembled, yet my heart swelled with certainty. With reverence, I lifted Amariah's small body from the shimmering box and placed her on the bed. Kneeling beside her, I whispered a prayer, my hands trembling with faith.

With firm conviction, I said:

Amariah, in the name of Jesus, arise.

Silence.

Then—a flutter. Her eyelids stirred. Slowly, she sat up. Her gaze met mine, her eyes shining with life. A radiant smile spread across her face as she whispered, *Mommy*.

Tears poured down my cheeks as I pulled her into my arms, feeling the warmth of her body, the miracle unfolding. Jesus smiled, his robe glowing with light. "Take Amariah and walk in the authority and victory I have given you. Share this miracle."

And just like that, we were back on the highway.

Amariah leapt from my arms, running toward her sister. Michaela gasped, her eyes wide. "Mom, where were you? We've been searching for you!"

Around us, medics and police officers stood frozen, staring at Amariah, baffled by the impossible.

"How is she alive?" they asked. "What happened?"

Before I could answer, a medic grabbed my arm. "Ma'am, help us," she pleaded. "We need your assistance with the other critically injured children. Do for them what you did for your daughter."

I stepped forward, my heart steady, my purpose clear.

And then—I woke up.

The dream lingered. Its meaning elusive. Its weight immense.

What is God trying to tell me?

For months, I kept it hidden—afraid of what others might think, unsure of its purpose. Was Amariah's suffering meant to bring healing to others? Did the school bus symbolize something greater? Why had Michaela—the one rushing to save others—been spared?

And why was I given the power to bring Amariah back?

The questions tormented me. But one thing was clear: this vision was no ordinary dream.

It was a calling.

Chapter 1

A Hopeful Journey

"May the God of hope fill you with all joy and peace as you trust in him."
— Romans 15:13

Hope isn't just wishful thinking—it's the unwavering trust that God is at work, even when things seem impossible. Every step of my journey required faith, a deep belief that God was present, guiding me, and filling my heart with hope.

I n early April 2010, I teetered on the edge of death. It happened suddenly—one moment I was standing in my church congregation in Somerville, Tennessee, my parents' hometown, and the next, everything faded into darkness. The doctors later described my survival as sheer luck, their voices laced with disbelief. But I knew better. It wasn't luck that pulled me back—it was something far greater. It was the amazing grace and power of God, reaching into the void and guiding me back to life.

In the weeks that followed, the weight of that experience lingered, shaping every thought and decision. My body had survived, but my spirit felt restless, craving renewal—a fresh beginning. Memorial Day weekend was approaching, and the idea of a road trip with the kids to Hampton Roads, Virginia began to take root in my heart. We needed to get away—needed laughter, open roads, something different. I told myself it was just a trip, but deep down, I knew it was more than that. I was seeking refuge.

Haywood County, Tennessee had already dismissed the kids for summer break, their laughter and freedom spilling into the long, sun-drenched days. With no rigid schedules to anchor us, the weight of urgency faded. I had the flexibility to make decisions without the pressure of a ticking clock.

A part of me held onto that thought, turning it over in my mind like a quiet reassurance. If Virginia ended up feeling like home again—like something I could settle into—I wanted the option to stay. I didn't want to feel rushed or forced into a decision before I was ready. This trip wasn't just about a change of scenery—it was about possibility. About leaving the door open to something different.

And so, in late spring of 2010, I packed up, leaving Haywood County behind and heading toward Hampton Roads—toward reconciliation. My estranged husband welcomed me back with open arms, his smile warm, his presence reassuring. For a moment, I allowed myself to believe that maybe—just maybe—this was the new beginning I had been praying for.

For a while, everything felt perfect. We slipped into an easy rhythm—days spent at the beach, the scent of salt and sunscreen lingering in the air as laughter echoed between crashing waves. His children from his previous marriage soon arrived for the summer, their presence blending seamlessly with our own. For a fleeting moment, we looked like the picture of a happy family—the kind I had longed to rebuild.

Then one afternoon, just as I was gathering towels and sunscreen for another trip to the shore, my phone buzzed in my hand. It was Pastor Wright from my church in Somerville. A warmth spread through me at the sight of his name, and I answered with enthusiasm.

"Hey, Pastor Wright!"

"Sister Tappe! How's it going?" His voice carried its usual joy, a familiarity that instantly put me at ease.

"It's going great! Just getting ready to take the kids to the beach."

"To the beach?" He paused for a moment. "Where are you?"

"I'm in Virginia, Pastor Wright. My estranged husband and I decided to reconcile during my Memorial Day visit."

Silence stretched between us before he finally responded. "Really? Well, okay. God wants families together. But I've got to admit, Sister Tappe, I feel like this is a bit premature. Are you sure?"

The certainty I had been clinging to suddenly felt fragile, but I pressed on. "Yes, I'm sure. He seems better this time."

Pastor Wright exhaled, his tone soft but weighted with concern. "I have to be honest, Sister Tappe. I don't think you gave it enough time. You haven't been separated quite a year. And you returned to Virginia—maybe it would have been better to let him come to you, to Tennessee, where you and the kids were."

I grew quiet, my fingers tightening around the phone. I had expected his encouragement, but instead, his words nudged at the uneasy feelings I had been trying to ignore.

"Look, I don't mean to discourage you," he continued, gentle but firm. "But as your Pastor, I've watched your growth over the past months. I just want to see you and the children succeed. You just recovered from a near-death experience, Sister Tappe. You've been through so much. Honestly, I just don't feel like your husband has truly changed."

A lump formed in my throat, thick and unrelenting. "I understand, Pastor Wright. I'm just trying to keep my family together. I appreciate your concern," I said, though my voice wavered.

"Well, I pray that all turns out well. I'll be praying for you and the children. Call me if you need me, and let me know if you plan to return soon."

I forced a swift response. "I will, Pastor Wright. Thank you."

As I ended the call, I stood frozen, the phone still pressed against my palm. His words echoed in my mind, stirring something deep within me. Maybe he was right. Maybe I had returned too soon.

But doubt is a dangerous thing, and I wasn't ready to let it take hold. I swallowed hard, forcing down the knot in my throat and the anxiety rising in my chest.

Maybe—just maybe—I was overthinking things.

As late October 2010 approached, I found myself immersed in planning my oldest daughter's third birthday party. The house buzzed with excitement—balloons, invitations, and the sweet anticipation of seeing her tiny face light up when she saw the cake decorated just for her. But beneath the surface, something felt off.

My husband, who had once been so present, so eager to be involved, suddenly seemed distant. His absence wasn't glaring—it was subtle, creeping in like a shadow stretching across our days. He wasn't offering to help with the preparations and barely acknowledged the party at all. At first, I chalked it up to stress, to distraction. But then came the nitpicking.

The smallest things set him off. A simple act of washing his laundry became an accusation: "Why are you washing my underwear?" The question caught me off guard—sharp, unwarranted. Another time, as I walked through the bedroom while he dressed after a shower, he stiffened, his voice clipped as he questioned why I was even in the room.

These weren't just random irritations—they were symptoms of something deeper, something I recognized all too well. My gut stirred with unease, an instinct whispering what my heart wasn't ready to accept. I had seen this behavior before—the sudden shift in mood, the withdrawal, the hypersensitivity to my presence. Before, it had signaled the unraveling of our marriage, leading to our prior separation. And now, as I stood surrounded by birthday decorations and mounting tension, I couldn't shake the feeling that someone else had entered the picture again.

My mind began to spiral, thoughts looping in restless circles. Anxiety crept in, settling into my chest like an unwelcome weight. *Not again,* I thought, my pulse quickening. I didn't want to relive the same painful cycle—the one that had driven me to Tennessee just a year before.

Yet despite my hesitation, my instincts whispered the truth I wasn't ready to face. The signs were there, familiar and undeniable. Something was shifting, unraveling beneath the surface. But how was I supposed to confront it? How could I find the right words when my heart was tangled in uncertainty?

By the beginning of November, the warmth that once held our home together had vanished, replaced by a suffocating coldness. His smiles grew scarce, his words clipped—each conversation reduced to bare, impersonal exchanges. The man I had reconciled with just months before had become a stranger in his own home, his presence now a lingering shadow of what it once was.

The air between us felt thick, weighted with the tension of things left unsaid. I could feel the ground shifting beneath me, the foundation I had tried so desperately to rebuild beginning to crack.

One evening, beneath the dim glow of the living room lamp, I finally gathered my courage. "What's wrong? Why have you been acting this way?" My voice carried more uncertainty than I intended, but I needed an answer.

His expression darkened. "Nothing's wrong. Just leave it alone," he muttered, refusing to meet my eyes.

And just like that, the conversation was over before it had begun.

The silence between us stretched long, growing heavier by the day. His late nights became routine—his excuses piling up like neglected debris. Rehearsals, projects, work—each one taking him further and further away. My calls went unanswered. My texts, ignored. The distance grew, tangible and painful.

Many nights, I lay awake, listening for the familiar click of the door unlocking, only to watch him stumble in at 2 a.m., exhaustion masking whatever truth he refused to speak.

"I'm too tired to talk," he would mumble before retreating into the bedroom, leaving me alone—alone with my doubts, my growing realization that something was irreparably breaking.

A few days later, he arrived home late again. This time, I wasn't going to let the silence stand between us.

It was past 2 a.m. when I asked, "Did one of your venues run late again?"

He ignored the question, brushing past me without a glance.

A swell of frustration pushed me to follow him into the bedroom, determination overriding the exhaustion weighing me down.

"Is there something we need to discuss? Are you unhappy, Rashard?" My voice was steady, though my heart thundered in my chest.

Nothing could have prepared me for what came next.

His response was delivered with cold arrogance, the words slicing through me like a blade.

"I'm not happy. I am in love with someone else."

Silence crashed down, thick and suffocating.

I didn't ask who—there was no need. The questionable texts on his phone from days prior had already whispered the truth I hadn't wanted to face.

As he rose from the bed and wandered back into the living room, something inside me crumbled.

Anxiety consumed my thoughts, clawing through my mind like a storm I couldn't outrun.

And then—then came the weight of something darker.

Depression trickled into my soul, quiet and unrelenting.

My worst fear had been confirmed.

Again.

Chapter 2

A New Journey

"Behold, I am doing a new thing; now it springs forth, do you not perceive it?"
Isaiah 43:19

Change is never easy, especially when life takes unexpected turns. This verse became my reminder that new beginnings are often hidden in the most difficult transitions. God was not abandoning me—He was leading me into something greater.

A week before Thanksgiving, exhaustion clung to me like a heavy fog. I was sleeping more than usual, dragging myself out of bed only to realize I was running late for work again. The fatigue was relentless, pressing down on me with an intensity I couldn't shake. *Maybe I'm just depressed,* I thought, still reeling from Rashard's confession that he had been seeing his ex-girlfriend again.

Then, in the middle of yet another rushed morning, a thought crept in—sharp and undeniable: *When was the last time you had a period, Tappe?*

I froze, mentally retracing the weeks, the days, the moments that had slipped by unnoticed. A realization hit—I was three weeks late. My stomach tightened, uncertainty pooling in my chest.

Without hesitation, I drove to the local drugstore. My footsteps were brisk, my breath uneven as I grabbed two packs of pregnancy tests. The familiar weight of anxiety settled over me as I made my way home, the box gripped tightly in my hands.

In the bathroom, under the unflinching light, I lined up the tests, one after another. I watched as the results appeared—bold, unwavering, undeniable. Four tests. Four confirmations. The truth stared back at me, offering no alternative.

For a moment, I felt nothing. Just quiet acceptance, as if my body already knew before my mind did.

Then—panic.

It crashed over me, wild and consuming. This pregnancy was arriving at the worst possible time—dropping into my life amid the wreckage. I had just been laid off, the second blow after struggling to recover from another job loss in Tennessee. My financial security was slipping through my fingers, my marriage fraying at the edges, unraveling faster than I could hold it together.

And now, there was life growing inside me—a reality I could not ignore, no matter how unsteady the ground beneath me felt.

I wasn't sure how to approach my now once-again estranged husband with the news. His recent confession—his rekindled connection with his ex-girlfriend—still echoed in my mind, sharp and unforgiving. The thought of announcing a pregnancy felt like pouring gasoline on a fire already burning out of control. Yet, no matter how much I wanted to avoid it, this was something I would have to face.

So one afternoon, when he came home from work, I steadied myself and sat down beside him on the couch, bracing for the inevitable.

"Rashard, I wanted to let you know that my period is over three weeks late," I began, my voice deliberate, measured. "So I went to the drugstore and got some pregnancy tests. I took four of them." I exhaled slowly. "They all came out positive."

I watched his face closely, searching for something—anything—that resembled emotion. Some flicker of concern or even mild curiosity. But his reaction was ice-cold. His eyes flared with a strange mix of fire and detachment, followed by a silence so thick I could feel its weight pressing between us.

Trying to push through the void, I continued. "I'm going to need to start prenatal care as soon as possible. So I was going to ask about your insurance."

His response came without hesitation, flat and unyielding.

"The kids and you are not on my insurance."

The words landed like a brutal strike to my chest.

I blinked, my mind scrambling to process his indifference. "Why aren't the kids and I on your insurance?" My voice trembled as I searched his face for an explanation, a reason—anything that might soften the blow.

He wouldn't meet my gaze.

"I forgot," he muttered, his posture slack, his shoulders slumping as he looked away.

The lack of remorse, the sheer carelessness of his words, sent a wave of frustration crashing over me, followed quickly by panic.

"What am I supposed to do now?" I whispered, my voice raw and desperate. "We have a baby on the way. I need prenatal care."

His chair scraped against the floor as he pushed it back, his movements slow, deliberate—detached. He stood, his presence looming for just a moment before he turned and walked away, abandoning the conversation.

Abandoning me.

I sat there, staring at the empty chair, my thoughts racing. How had everything fallen apart so quickly?

As the days passed, the divide between us deepened, each unspoken word carving a wider canyon of separation. He made it clear—he was uncertain about our marriage, uncertain about everything. His nights out became more frequent. His routine shifted—new habits replacing the old. He spoke of work events, of nights spent with friends, always leaving a little earlier, returning a little later.

And every evening, as I waited in silence, the unbearable truth settled deeper into my soul:

This was no longer home.

By the time I realized I was at least eight weeks pregnant, the weight of uncertainty had settled deep into my bones. Anxiety gnawed at me, relentless and unyielding. Each day without prenatal care felt like a ticking clock—a silent reminder of how fragile everything had become.

Desperate for a solution, I applied for Medicaid, only to find myself entangled in a maze of paperwork and bureaucratic red tape. Every form and requirement seemed like another wall between me and the care I so urgently needed. Even after maneuvering through it all, my approval still depended on one final step: the official pregnancy confirmation from the local health department.

But securing that appointment proved just as difficult. Each phone call brought another delay. Every available slot seemed to vanish before I could claim it. The waiting was maddening.

Finally, on the day before New Year's Eve, I found myself in the crowded waiting room of the health department. Around me, bright streamers and glittering ornaments clung to the walls—leftovers of the holiday season. They should have brought warmth and comfort. Instead, they felt out of place, their cheerfulness stark against the weight that pressed on my chest.

Outside, the world prepared to welcome a new year with laughter and fireworks. But I sat in stillness, wrapped in anxiety, waiting for news I wasn't sure I was ready to receive.

Then a nurse called my name. Her voice, kind and warm, felt like a brief release from the tightness inside me. When I stepped forward, she greeted me with a smile that almost made me breathe easier.

"How are you feeling?" she asked gently.

"I'm okay... but not the greatest," I admitted, managing a small smile. "The morning sickness has been pretty rough."

Her face softened. "I'm sorry you're not feeling well," she said, gently rubbing my upper arm—a small gesture, but one that helped ease the weight just a little.

"I'm going to take a few vials of blood," she explained. "We need to confirm some things for both my records and your caseworker's—for your Medicaid application. Just relax."

She worked quickly and carefully, her hands confident as she searched for a vein. "I'm tying this armband," she said. "Hold this ball for me while I work. Then we'll go from there, okay?"

I nodded, swallowing hard, trying to push past the nerves lodged in my throat.

As she prepared the supplies, I took a deep breath, willing myself to stay calm. This moment—this appointment—was more than routine. It was real now. Not just two pink lines on a stick, not just a private worry whispered to myself. This was my first real step forward.

The nurse, her eyes soft with compassion, handed me the results.

"Congratulations, you're expecting," she said with a gentle brightness. "Your baby is due around July 15th."

I swallowed again, my voice barely above a whisper. "How long until my Medicaid is approved?"

"It can take up to forty-five days in Virginia," she said, sympathy in her tone. "Unfortunately, that might mean you won't begin prenatal care until after the twelve-week mark."

Forty-five days.

I nodded, managing a small smile, though everything inside me felt tight and uncertain.

That timeline stretched ahead of me like a foggy road I couldn't see the end of.

Chapter 3

A Journey of Loneliness

"The Lord is close to the brokenhearted and saves those who are crushed in spirit."
– Psalm 34:18

Loneliness has a way of creeping in, making you feel unseen and forgotten. But this verse reminded me that God was near, even in the depths of my sorrow. He was present in the silence, in the moments when all I had were my tears—whispering that I was never truly alone.

During this incredibly challenging time in my life, I found solace in the grace of God and the support of my church family. My co-pastor checked in on me from time to time, asking how my marriage was holding up. She and her husband, our senior pastor, had previously provided individual marriage counseling for my husband and me a few years before the separation. Unfortunately, my husband had grown increasingly resistant and had refused to speak to the senior pastor any further. Still, my co-pastor and I never stopped communicating.

After noticing my absence from church for several Sundays, she gave me a call.

"Hey, I missed you at church these past few weeks. Is everything okay?" she asked, her voice filled with genuine concern.

I took a deep breath and replied, "I recently found out I'm pregnant, and the hyperemesis is really kicking in."

"Oh, congratulations!" she exclaimed warmly. "Children are such a blessing from the Lord."

Her kind words brought a small smile to my face, but she sensed there was more behind the silence.

"How's the reconciliation with your husband going? How does he feel about the pregnancy?" she asked gently.

I hesitated before admitting, "Things aren't going as expected. He isn't thrilled about the pregnancy." My voice trembled as I continued, "And... I think he's seeing his ex-girlfriend again."

The moment those words escaped, I broke down in tears.

"I'm so sorry you're going through this," she said softly, her voice soothing my aching heart. "But remember, it's going to be okay. You are strong, and you have us to support you."

Then came the invitation my spirit desperately needed.

"Come by the church for our New Year's Eve party. Bring the children. Don't spend tonight alone. Don't let the enemy pull you into isolation and depression."

"I'll come," I promised. "Just give me about thirty to forty-five minutes to get the kids and myself ready and head over."

Thankfully, my church was only ten minutes away. Despite the biting December cold and the fatigue from hyperemesis, my need for comfort and community outweighed the discomfort.

As I bundled up the kids and prepared to leave, a flicker of hope sparked in my heart. In the middle of all the chaos, I wasn't completely alone.

When we arrived at the church, my co-pastor greeted me with a warm hug.

"It's so good to see you and the kids," she said, her eyes shining with kindness. "I'm going to have the youth pastor take them to enjoy some movies and pizza, just to give you some momma time. Is that okay?"

"Yes," I said with a heavy sigh, the exhaustion evident in my voice. Tears welled up in my eyes. "I really appreciate that, Pastor K."

"Of course," she replied with a compassionate smile. "That's what a church family is for."

The youth pastor approached and gently took my daughter and son by the hand. As they walked away, I watched them go with a mix of gratitude and relief.

I found a seat in the sanctuary, my emotions still raw and swirling. Some of the church members noticed me and came over with warm hugs and friendly hellos. Their kindness brought a flicker of life to my weary heart.

The senior pastor preached passionately about leaving the past behind in 2010 and embracing new beginnings in 2011. His words rang with hope and promise, and as he spoke, something began to stir in me. Though my mind swirled with questions about the future, his message cut through the noise.

Silently, I cried out to God, "How am I going to get what I need for the baby? Where will we live? How will I find the strength to finish college?"

The weight of it all pressed heavily on me. But as the pastor continued to speak, his words began to pierce the fog in my heart. He spoke about faith, about God's renewal, about moving forward even when the path isn't clear.

Somehow, something shifted. I felt the stirrings of a new vision, a new sense of courage. Faith began to rise, washing over the anxious thoughts about money, my emotional state, and the challenges ahead. I felt a sense of release, a quiet assurance that with God's help, I could face whatever the new year held.

Suddenly, I became curious about the time. I turned and looked up at the black analog wall clock above the sanctuary door. As I watched the hand sweep through the final minutes of the year, I congratulated myself for finding the strength to come. I was proud. In my heart, I knew God was proud of me too.

And I thanked Him for speaking to Pastor K's heart, for making that phone call, and for leading me into this place of peace.

As Pastor wrapped up his message, I glanced at the clock—it was just five minutes to midnight.

"Will you please stand as we prepare our hearts to enter into 2012?" he said fervently, motioning with his hands.

I rose from the shiny brown pew and looked around. Suddenly, it hit me: every member seated had a significant other beside them—except me.

A quiet ache filled my chest.

My heart whispered to God, *What's so wrong with me that my supposed significant other doesn't even want to bring in the new year with me? Why am I the only woman here standing alone—and pregnant, on top of that?*

The thoughts came fast and heavy, pressing down until tears threatened to fall. As the congregation began the countdown, voices rose in unison.

"Five, four, three, two, one—Happy New Year!"

The sanctuary erupted in celebration—tears of joy, laughter, a sea of warm hugs and heartfelt wishes passed from one person to another. I watched the outpouring of love around me and felt deeply grateful to be among my church family. Their warmth offered a brief but needed shelter from the coldness of my own solitude.

Around 2 a.m., I gathered the kids and prepared to leave the haven of the church. My pastor and her husband walked us to the car, their presence steady and kind. The night air was cold and sharp, but their care felt like a comforting balm against it. Pastor Kay hugged me tightly.

"I'll give you a call shortly," she said gently, her voice carrying genuine care.

When we arrived at our dark and quiet duplex, the silence was stark. It was such a contrast to the joy-filled noise we had just left behind. I began settling the kids when my phone rang.

Pastor Kay's voice came through, warm and reassuring.

"Praise God! I'm so glad to know you and the kids made it home safely. Make sure you all rest up today. We'll touch bases soon."

"Thanks, Pastor Kay. We had a great time. I didn't realize just how much we all needed to get out tonight," I replied, my gratitude pouring through the line. "Thanks for thinking of us. We'll talk soon."

Within ten minutes of ending the call, exhaustion swept over me like a wave. As I sank into bed, a peace I hadn't felt in so long settled around me like a soft blanket.

For the first time in what felt like forever, I rested.

Prevailing Prayer

A few days later, the morning sun filtered softly through the curtains as I stirred awake. I noticed my youngest son, Richon, rummaging through the refrigerator, his little face scrunched with worry.

"Mom, what are we going to eat for the rest of the week?" he asked, his voice laced with concern.

I got up and joined him, peering into the nearly empty fridge. "Let's see," I said, trying to sound hopeful. Inside, there was some bread, a gallon of milk, a couple of gallons of water, and a few slices of cheese. A couple of half-empty boxes of cereal sat on the shelf. Not exactly a feast.

Richon's eyes met mine, searching for something solid in the midst of uncertainty.

"Don't worry, son," I said softly. "Go ahead and eat breakfast. I'll figure something out."

As he prepared his cereal, I felt that all-too-familiar gnawing worry settle in. I was pregnant, unemployed, and navigating a broken marriage. Our resources were running low, and I didn't yet have the answers.

I decided to take Richon to school and told myself I'd work something out when I got back. On the drive, I prayed quietly, my heart aching for clarity and strength, trusting that somehow, God would meet us where we were.

Back at home, I settled my daughter in front of one of her favorite Tinker Bell movies. Her eyes sparkled with joy as the screen lit up.

"Mommy's going to talk to Jesus for a little while, okay? Stay here and be a good girl," I whispered.

She nodded eagerly. "Okay, Mommy!"

I walked into the bedroom, and as soon as my knees hit the floor, tears streamed down my face. The weight of everything I had been carrying became too much.

"Thank you, God, for your goodness and mercy," I cried. "Thank you for allowing me and my kids to wake up this morning."

My voice trembled, but I pressed on.

"Thank you for all you have done for us, for what you're doing now, and for what you're going to do. I'm grateful for your presence in our lives."

I paused, my breathing uneven, and then began to speak His promises back to Him.

"You said in Psalm 23 that You are my Shepherd—I shall not want. And in Psalm 121, You said I can lift my eyes to the hills, and my help will come from You. And in Philippians 4:19, You promised to supply all my needs according to Your riches in glory."

"God, these are Your words. You've never failed me. I'm unemployed, pregnant, and in an estranged marriage. I'm preparing to leave this house and move in with my sister. But Your Word says the earth is Yours, and everything in it. You can't lie—it's impossible for You to lie."

Desperation rose in my voice.

"Please, open the door of provision. Speak to the heart of one of Your servants. Send supernatural help so I can feed my son and daughter. Thank You, Father, in advance. In Jesus' name, Amen."

Later that afternoon, I picked up Richon from school. As soon as we got home, he dropped his backpack and hurried to the fridge, scanning the contents.

"Mom, I thought you said you were going to the grocery store," he said, his voice tinged with quiet worry.

I sighed and steadied my voice.

"I will soon, sweetheart. There's something we're waiting on, and it will come. Don't worry, okay? Just have your sandwich, drink your juice, and enjoy some snacks with your sister. It'll be alright. God won't let us go hungry. Just be patient while we wait."

He nodded, though concern still lingered in his eyes. Michaela, carefree as always, munched away happily beside him.

Not long after, my phone rang. It was Pastor Kay.

"Hi, Pastor. Is everything okay?" I asked.

"Hello, dear. I wanted to know if you could stop by the church tonight."

My brow furrowed. "There's no service tonight—why do I need to come?"

She paused before answering, "I know there's no service, but I don't know if I ever mentioned—we have a food pantry at the church. While I was there praying and working earlier today, God told me to set some food aside just for you and the kids. But you'll need to come and get it."

My jaw dropped. Tears flooded my eyes.

"Are you crying? What's wrong?" she asked gently.

Through my sobs, I replied, "Yes, I'm crying. Pastor Kay, I was praying earlier today, asking God for help—because we need food. My Medicaid and food EBT haven't come through yet. I told Jesus everything, just like my parents taught me."

"Wow," she said in amazement. "Look at God. Isn't He something?"

"Yes, He is!" I exclaimed. "He placed you on my heart while I was pouring mine out to Him. Thank You, Jesus. This confirms everything."

"Get yourself and the kids ready and come on over. Do you have enough gas?"

"I have a little."

"Okay. When you get here, I'll help you with that too. We'll get you squared away. See you soon."

"Thank you so much, Pastor Kay."

"No problem, dear. See you soon."

Upon arriving at the church, Pastor Kay welcomed us with a warm, tight hug.

"It's so good to see you," she said, leading us through the sanctuary. We passed the new convert section and the overflow area before entering a hallway. At the end of it, she opened a door to a room with light blue walls, brightly lit like an elementary classroom. Shelves lined the space, stocked with boxes of grains, canned goods, and rows of kids' juice boxes, snacks, and loaves of bread. The room was nearly filled to capacity.

"Wow, Pastor Kay," I said, wide-eyed. "I never even knew this room existed. When did this happen?"

She smiled while gathering items into a box. "We opened this food pantry ministry last year, in 2010. God blessed us with donations from so many sources. We saw a need—and God made a way. So far, it's been a blessing."

"That's wonderful," I replied. "I've always believed no one should go hungry. Life brings many challenges, but hunger shouldn't be one of them."

"Agreed," she said, nodding.

Within minutes, Pastor Kay called over Associate Minister Pastor Thoreau. He greeted me with his usual cheerful, "Hey, Sister Tappe."

"Hi, Pastor Thoreau. How's it going? How's your wife?"

"Doing good today," he replied in his Creole accent, flashing a wide grin. "My wife's doing just fine. I'll tell her you asked after her. Pastor Kay says all of this is going to you," he said, pointing to four tall boxes. "So, where's your car?"

"It's the little red four-door Mazda sedan out in the parking lot," I said.

"It's freezing out there, and I see you're pregnant. Why don't you and the kids stay here where it's warm? Hand me your keys—I'll load everything into the car. How 'bout that?"

"Sure, Pastor Thoreau. I really appreciate it."

"Good. I'll be back in about ten minutes and get you squared away."

While he moved the boxes to my car, Pastor Kay kept the kids entertained with snacks and small activities so we could talk privately. We sat at a nearby table where she handed me an envelope with cash.

"Look, I know you didn't ask for this," she said gently, "but I wanted to give you a little something for gas and personal items. I just want to do what God told me to do."

Tears flowed like a river.

"Pastor Kay, I don't even know what to say except thank you. You're the answer to a prayer. I was praying to God after taking my son to school this morning. He's been worried about the food situation, and I didn't know how I was going to make it happen—but I believed God wouldn't leave us without help. Then you called, and everything changed. I'm speechless. I truly know God loves us."

She placed a comforting hand on my shoulder.

"Of course He loves you. This is just a season. It'll pass, and you'll come through it stronger. Right now, He's giving you daily bread. He's teaching you to trust Him—because for the road ahead, you'll need to trust Him without hesitation."

"I believe that. I don't know everything that's ahead, but I know it's going to be a long road."

Just then, Pastor Thoreau returned, his voice bright. "All done! Let's get you and the kids out to the car and home from this cold weather."

Together, Pastor Kay, Pastor Thoreau, the children, and I walked to the parking lot. They reminded me to call or text once we made it home.

After leaving the church, I stopped briefly to fill up the tank of my Mazda 626. It took less than ten minutes. About five minutes later, we pulled into the driveway.

My son's eyes widened as he saw the boxes.

"Was this what you were waiting for, Mom?"

"Not exactly," I said with a smile. "I was waiting for something else, but after I picked you up, Pastor Kay called and asked me to come by the church. Either way, I'm grateful. God is good."

"I'm loving all the snacks, Mommy!" Michaela said excitedly.

"I bet you are, little lady," I replied.

"Yay! Thank you, Jesus!" she shouted like a little cheerleader.

We spent about 30 to 45 minutes sorting through the food. There was enough to last us two to three weeks. It warmed my heart to know I could finally feed my children well—and nourish my growing body. At 15 weeks pregnant, I needed the strength and nutrition.

Later that night, after putting the children to bed, I got down on my knees to thank God. I prayed with my whole heart, praising Him for about thirty minutes. I thanked Him for stepping in so powerfully. When I finally lay down, I slept soundly—the best sleep I'd had in weeks.

The next morning, I called social services and asked to speak to my case worker, Mrs. Williams. To my surprise, she was available.

"Good morning, Mrs. Williams," I greeted, trying to keep my anxiety hidden.

"Good morning," she replied calmly.

"I haven't received any communication since submitting my application and attending the pregnancy test. Could you provide me with an update on my status?" I asked.

"Sure," she said. "I'm going to place you on a brief hold, okay?"

"Sure," I replied, the knot in my stomach tightening. The minutes felt long, though only five passed before she returned.

"Ma'am, your EBT and Medicaid cards are here. They've been here for about two weeks. Didn't our intake team contact you?" she asked, surprised.

"No, ma'am," I replied, frustration slipping into my voice.

"I'm so sorry about that," she said sincerely. "They were supposed to call you when everything came in. Your items are being held at the front desk—right where you submitted your application. You've been approved for Medicaid due to your pregnancy, and there's a substantial balance on your EBT card, retroactive to your application date of December 23, 2010. You can come pick them up at any time."

"Thank you so much, Mrs. Williams. I need to secure prenatal care as soon as possible. I'll be in shortly," I said, relief washing over me.

Chapter 4

A Journey of Strength

*"I can do all things through Christ
who strengthens me."*
– Philippians 4:13

There were days I felt weak, uncertain of how I would keep going. Strength wasn't something I could muster on my own—it had to come from Him. When I surrendered my fears, I discovered that His strength was enough, carrying me through challenges I never imagined overcoming.

Eventually, I moved in with my sister after my marriage fell apart. My ex no longer wanted to be around me. He admitted—bluntly—that he was unhappy, that his feelings for me had faded, and that he was in love with someone else. His words were sharp and final. They cut deep, but they also marked the start of a new chapter: one of survival.

The kids and I relocated to my younger sister's apartment. It was a significant adjustment. The space was small, stripped of the familiar comforts we once knew. Still, it offered something far greater—peace. There were no nearby friends, no close-knit community to fall back on, just my sister, the one person willing to stand by us. As I tried to settle into our new reality, the loneliness pressed in like a heavy fog.

Then came another blow. My Medicaid approval finally came through—too late. I was already 16 weeks pregnant, and the sinking feeling in my chest was instant. My first call to an OB-GYN's office ended in rejection.

"I'm sorry," the receptionist said. "We can't accept patients this far along without prior care."

Each rejection added to my fear and frustration. Would anyone help me? Night after night, I lay awake with my hand resting on my growing belly, the weight of uncertainty heavier than ever.

Then, in what felt like a divine answer to my silent prayers, a CMS representative called me back for a prenatal care follow-up. Her voice was calm and concerned as I explained how unsafe I felt, how I'd been turned away repeatedly, and how the discrimination I had experienced left me questioning where I could turn.

She listened patiently, then asked me to hold while she did some research. Minutes passed, stretching into what felt like hours. I held onto hope like a lifeline, silently praying that someone—anyone—would be willing to take me in.

Finally, she returned with good news: two doctors who specialized in high-risk and late prenatal care and were open to taking on special cases.

The first was a highly experienced African American male doctor, over seventy and well-established in the field. The second was a younger African American female OB-GYN, closer to my age.

With cautious optimism, I scheduled an appointment with the male doctor. Still, uncertainty lingered—an uneasiness I couldn't shake.

That uncertainty followed me right up until the day of my sonogram. As I stepped into the younger OB-GYN's facility, something shifted. The environment felt different—welcoming, warm, reassuring. The staff was attentive and compassionate in a way I hadn't expected. It was clear in how they spoke to each patient, how they moved with intention.

It was in that moment that I knew—I was in the right place.

And then I met Dr. Nicole—the doctor who would change everything.

Her reputation preceded her, but meeting her confirmed what I already sensed. She was highly recommended, deeply compassionate, and fiercely committed to her patients. That day, I made a decision: I wouldn't return to the previous OB-GYN.

Dr. Nicole was exactly who I needed. She would transform my pregnancy experience in ways I hadn't imagined.

Finding an Advocate

At 24 weeks, I was classified as high-risk and required continuous monitoring. My initial care had been with the elderly male OB-GYN. He was experienced, yes—but I needed something more. I needed a different kind of care—one rooted not only in expertise but in understanding and empathy.

That's when I returned to Dr. Nicole's facility.

From the moment I walked into her office, I felt it again—that undeniable sense of belonging and peace. Her staff's attentiveness was reassuring, and her practice felt like a place where patients were truly seen—not just for their physical symptoms, but for the fullness of their lives.

I requested to switch doctors. To my surprise, the transition was smooth and swift. I took it as a divine sign—confirmation that I was exactly where I was meant to be.

From the very first visit, Dr. Nicole was thorough. She assessed every aspect of my health and life. She didn't just ask about my pregnancy—she asked about my mental well-being, the health of my baby, even whether I had reliable transportation. She understood the weight of my circumstances, and she never minimized my experience.

She became my greatest advocate. A steady, consistent presence through every twist and turn. At each appointment, she paid close attention—not only to my charts and test results but to the person behind them. She knew about my strained marriage and everything I carried emotionally. But she never judged. She only offered compassion and guidance when I needed it most.

Her presence wasn't just clinical—it was comforting. Grounding. A lifeline when I felt like I was drowning.

The Fight for Stability

After Memorial Day, summer arrived with an unforgiving intensity. June and July were drenched in heat, and hydration became a daily battle—a relentless effort made even harder by my hyperemesis.

To support a healthy pregnancy, Dr. Nicole gave me three essential tasks:

- Take 50,000 IU of Vitamin D as prescribed
- Manage hyperemesis with medication as needed
- Walk regularly to relieve stress

But the most crucial of them all was water—64 to 80 ounces each day, a non-negotiable lifeline for both my baby and me.

Some days, reaching that goal felt like chasing the horizon—always necessary, yet painfully out of reach. My body was already at war with itself. Nausea hit in endless waves. Exhaustion wrapped around me like a weighted blanket. The stress of trying to stay afloat—physically, emotionally, spiritually—was constant. Even the act of drinking a few sips of water felt like climbing a mountain with no summit in sight.

Hyperemesis gravidarum wasn't just sickness—it was suffocating. I had faced it before with Michaela, but this time—with Amariah—it came harder, fiercer. It stripped me of functionality. I couldn't work. Leaving the house was a gamble, each step shadowed by dizziness and dry heaving. Standing upright for too long felt impossible, as though my body might give out at any moment. Even silence could be unbearable—every hum, every flicker of light, every smell turned into a trigger.

It was an isolating kind of suffering. Invisible to most, but consuming. And still—I pressed on.

I wasn't alone. My case management nurse became an unexpected source of strength. She sent me a water bottle and checked in regularly, a quiet accountability partner reminding me that support existed—even when it felt like the world had closed its doors.

A Birth on Its Own Terms

As my due date—July 13—approached, Dr. Nicole scheduled an induction for 9 AM. The plan was to welcome Amariah with intention and calm. Still, I told her, "My babies always come on their own time." She smiled and kept the appointment on the calendar, just in case.

And, just like that, my body had its say.

In the stillness before dawn, my water broke—suddenly, without warning—just before 3 AM. My heart pounded. This is happening. Now.

The hours that followed blurred into sharp contractions. They surged, relentless, swallowing the world around me. The hospital was overflowing—so many babies choosing that day to arrive. With no rooms available, I was told to walk through my labor until one opened up.

Each step was agony. I clung to hallway rails, breath ragged, teeth clenched, sweat beading on my skin. The pain far surpassed anything I remembered. I cried silent tears, prayed silent prayers. Just when I felt I couldn't walk another inch, a room became available—less than four hours before Amariah's birth. Grace, arriving right on time.

The pain intensified. I asked for an epidural, desperate for even a sliver of relief. By 3 PM, I felt her moving, descending slowly, surely. Every breath, every push, every ounce of strength poured into that final stretch.

And then, just before 4 PM—she came.

At first—stillness.

No cry. Just quiet urgency.

The room shifted. Nurses moved quickly but calmly. Their voices were soft, their hands steady. My heart stopped in my chest as I watched them surround her. I whispered prayers between each breath.

Then it came.

A loud, piercing cry split the silence. Her voice was raw and fierce and unmistakably alive. The sound of survival. Of purpose. Of a little girl arriving with fire and strength.

Dr. Nicole's team never left my side. Five women—each highly skilled, compassionate, personally trained by her. They moved like a unit, their knowledge seamless, their care unspoken but present. They guided me with wisdom, steadied me with kindness. They saw me not just as a patient but as a mother—fighting, enduring, hoping.

And then, Dr. Nicole walked in.

Her presence was steady, familiar, grounding. With a confident smile, she delivered the words I had prayed for: Amariah was healthy. She was strong. She had arrived safely despite every challenge.

From start to finish, Dr. Nicole and her team had been more than medical professionals—they had been a constant, quiet force. A net beneath me. An anchor in the storm.

A Life Changed

Through every obstacle—heartbreak, uncertainty, sickness, rejection, heat, fear—I had made it.

Not by chance. Not by medicine alone. But by God. By faith that held firm. By perseverance pulled from somewhere deep within. And by the unwavering strength of the people who stood beside me.

And now—she was here.

As I cradled Amariah for the first time, everything fell away. The pain. The tears. The nights I cried out to God. The rejections. The fear. All of it dissolved into that single, holy moment.

All that remained was love—pure, fierce, unshakable. And the quiet hum of victory in my chest.

She felt different.

There was something sacred in the way she fit against me. Something holy in the weight of her warmth. In the stillness that followed her first cry. It felt as if her soul had seen more than this world could yet understand.

It wasn't just the joy of holding new life.

It was the knowing—that her arrival meant something more. That she had come to shift things. That she would change lives—her siblings', mine, and those beyond our little family.

She was larger than the moment. Larger than the room. Larger, even, than me.

I couldn't explain it.

But I felt it.

With every fiber of my being.

Chapter 5

Navigating the Medical Journey

"But I will restore you to health and heal your wounds," declares the Lord.
— Jeremiah 30:17

Few experiences test the human spirit like a battle for health. This chapter unfolds the tension of medical uncertainty, the quiet frustration of not being heard, and the persistent faith that kept me grounded.

When Amariah turned one, I noticed something that didn't sit right with me. One of her top teeth—maybe a molar or incisor—came in chipped. Her bottom teeth carried a discoloration that seemed far too noticeable for a baby just entering toddlerhood.

At her one-year well-child exam, I voiced my concern.

"Doctor, I'm really worried about Amariah's teeth," I said, holding her close on my lap. "Her bottom teeth look discolored, and one of her top teeth came in chipped."

The pediatrician leaned in for a closer look, studying Amariah's tiny teeth with a thoughtful frown. "Hmm," she murmured. "I see what you're referring to."

"What does she typically drink?" she asked.

"She mostly drinks water, apple juice, and milk," I answered, hoping my response might ease my growing worry. "She also eats plenty of fruits and vegetables."

"Well, let's keep an eye on her juice and milk intake," she advised gently. "The sugar content can lead to early dental problems. If these issues persist until she's two, then it'll be time to consult a pediatric dentist. That's usually the age when most of them will begin seeing children."

As Amariah's second birthday approached, I made an appointment at a popular children's dental clinic. Their bright commercials promised a fun, playful environment, and both Amariah and Michaela were excited for the visit.

"Mommy, is this the place with the fun toys and the big slide?" Michaela asked, eyes gleaming.

"Yes, it is," I said, smiling. "And you'll get to see the dentist, too!"

Inside, I stayed cheerful for the kids' sake, but my spirit was heavy. Why was this happening to Amariah? None of my other children had dental issues this early. Quietly, I wrestled with questions for God—why her, and why now?

I scheduled cleanings for all my children—RJ (17), Richon (11), and Michaela (5). The dental hygienist greeted us warmly, offering smiles that eased some of my nervous energy.

"Do you have any concerns you'd like the doctor to know about?" she asked as we settled into the exam room.

"Yes, mainly about Amariah," I replied, gently helping her into the chair. "The chipped tooth seems to have healed, but there's still discoloration and what looks like decalcification on her upper teeth."

She nodded and noted my concerns.

After examining Amariah's teeth, the dentist said, "Let's monitor this for the next six months to a year. In the meantime, reduce juice, snacks, and sugary drinks. That's where these kinds of problems typically start."

A quiet frustration bubbled up inside me.

"I beg to differ, doctor," I said carefully. "She doesn't really drink much juice. Her snacks are mostly fruits and vegetables. Maybe two small cups of apple juice a day, nothing excessive. She's not consuming a lot of sugar."

He shook his head, unfazed. "In school, we're taught it's always in the diet, ma'am."

I blinked, feeling a familiar sting in my chest. "I'm not so sure that's the whole picture," I said, gently but firmly. "I think there might be another cause."

But he dismissed it, sticking to the textbook answer.

I left that appointment discouraged. I knew something was off, but I couldn't seem to get anyone to listen. The quiet doubt from the professionals—their unwillingness to consider alternatives—left me feeling helpless. I wasn't asking for magic. I was asking for someone to look deeper. To see what I saw.

I sought a second opinion, but the next pediatric dentist echoed the same view. Their words, though polite, carried an underlying message: this was your fault. And their prognosis left little room for hope.

Still, I didn't give up.

Every visit, I clung to the possibility that maybe things would turn around. But the discoloration and decalcification remained. And each time, the answer was the same: "We'll keep monitoring it."

My mother's heart ached with questions, but I refused to let fear dictate the story. I chose to trust the process—however slow, however uncertain—and to place Amariah's care in God's hands. He had carried us this far. He wouldn't leave us now.

Even in the silence of unanswered questions, I knew He was guiding her journey.

Reflections – Years Three and Four

By the end of 2014, my frustration with previous dentists had reached its peak. They kept telling me to simply monitor Amariah's teeth, but I knew deep down that something more needed to be done.

At the beginning of 2015, I booked an appointment with a new pediatric dentist, Dr. Micah McKenna. I didn't realize then that I was about to uncover another layer to this already complex issue.

Dr. Micah examined Amariah's teeth gently, her fingers moving with careful precision. She echoed the previous concerns about the white spots but offered something different—hope.

"These white spots are known as enamel hypoplasia," she explained, her voice calm and reassuring. "It's a form of demineralization. But we can work on strengthening the enamel over time. I'll create a plan we can follow over the next few months."

At one of our visits, Dr. Micah was out of the office, and a male doctor stepped in. I quickly noticed that he shared her last name. A hygienist confirmed my curiosity with a smile.

"Dr. Micah and her husband, Dr. Michael McKenna, started this practice together," she said. "She'll be going on maternity leave soon, so your daughter will be seeing her husband for a while."

Dr. Michael was kind and attentive. But his exam revealed something troubling.

"The enamel on one of Amariah's back teeth is very soft," he told me, concern evident in his eyes. "Extraction is the best route. Since it's a primary tooth, it will eventually be replaced."

My heart dropped. I wanted to trust his expertise, but my spirit bristled with unease.

Sensing my hesitation, Dr. Michael added, "We can monitor it for now, but I don't expect the tooth to improve. I truly believe extraction is the best course."

I paused and finally said, "I'll wait until Amariah's next treatment before deciding."

At her follow-up, he remained firm in his recommendation. My heart was still heavy, but against my better judgment, I gave in. I agreed to the procedure, hoping it was the right thing for her.

After the extraction, an unsettling feeling began to grow inside me. It wouldn't go away. The more time passed, the more uneasy I felt. Eventually, I confronted the office.

"Why didn't you try sealing her tooth instead of extracting it?" I asked, my voice tight with worry.

Dr. Michael shook his head. "With enamel that soft, sealing wouldn't have worked," he said with gentle finality. "Extraction was the best option."

Still, his response brought little peace. I tried to quiet my thoughts, but the weight of the decision stayed with me. My instincts whispered that there had to be another way—something less drastic.

I reached out to my mentor.

"I'm concerned about the extraction site," I told her. "Something doesn't sit right with me."

She nodded slowly. "I understand. You should definitely get a second opinion. A missing molar can affect how her permanent teeth come in later."

"You're right," I said, a sense of determination rising in me. "I'll look for another dentist."

That night, my thoughts spiraled into a familiar pattern of guilt. I lay awake, staring into the dark, questioning everything.

"Is this all my fault?" I whispered. "Did I do something wrong? Could I have prevented this?"

One by one, memories from my pregnancy resurfaced like waves—each one crashing into me with fresh force. The hyperemesis, the severe Vitamin D deficiency, the homelessness. Had those struggles led us here?

The guilt came fast and heavy, washing over me until I couldn't hold it in any longer. I wept—long, hot tears that felt like they'd been waiting years to fall.

"God," I cried, "I need answers. How can I fix this? How can I protect my children from the consequences of what I couldn't control?"

My voice broke under the weight of my emotion. I kept praying—pleading—for understanding, for strength, for peace.

Eventually, exhaustion took hold, and I drifted off in prayer. My heart still heavy, but my spirit still reaching.

Chapter 6

The Surgical Journey

"Do not fear, for I am with you; do not be dismayed, for I am your God."
— Isaiah 41:10

Facing surgery was one of the most frightening moments of my journey. But when fear threatened to overtake me, this verse kept me grounded. In every moment of uncertainty—in that bright, sterile operating room—God was present. His peace surrounded me in a way I cannot fully explain.

Meeting with the Specialist

In February 2016, I took my youngest daughter, Amariah, to see a new pediatric dentist. Her previous dentist had removed one of her back molars, and to say I was displeased would be an understatement. I couldn't quite put my finger on it at the time, but I felt deeply that something had been mishandled.

Amariah was only four and a half, still early in the process of losing baby teeth and growing her permanent ones. There was no infrastructure in place to hold the space where the missing tooth had been. A friend of mine strongly suggested we try a well-known pediatric dental practice in the Hampton Roads area, one that had cared for her own son until he turned 21.

"You should give them a try," she urged. "My son's 30 now and has never had a problem with his teeth."

I knew the practice's adult dentistry had a great reputation, but I hadn't heard much about their pediatric side. Her recommendation stayed with me. After a bit of research at home and confirming they were within my insurance network, I felt confident enough to move forward.

The next morning, I called.

"Good morning, I'd like to schedule a dental appointment for my daughter, Amariah," I said, trying to keep the urgency out of my voice.

"Of course," the receptionist said kindly. "We have an opening next Thursday at 10 a.m. Will that work for you?"

"Yes, that works perfectly. Thank you," I replied, feeling a mix of anticipation and relief.

When the day arrived, I felt both hopeful and anxious. Amariah had been through so much already. I just wanted answers—and solutions.

The clinic's atmosphere was immediately comforting. Bright colors danced across the walls, and the waiting area was filled with storybooks and toys. Amariah's face lit up the moment we walked in.

"Look, Mommy! They have my favorite books!" she squealed, dashing toward a shelf.

I smiled. "I'm glad you like it here, sweetie."

Though she was nervous from past dental experiences, the dentist's calming presence quickly put us both at ease.

"Hello, I'm Dr. David," he said warmly, extending a hand. "How are we doing today?"

"We're well, thank you," I replied. "I understand you were expecting us?"

"Yes, I've reviewed some notes. What brings you in?"

"My daughter recently had one of her molars pulled due to a cavity. While I agreed to it at the time, I've had some doubts. A friend recommended your office, and I'm hoping you can help clarify things."

Dr. David nodded thoughtfully, then adjusted the examining chair and gently had Amariah recline. As he and the assistants examined her teeth, I listened quietly as they exchanged numbers and terms in medical shorthand. The tone of their conversation told me everything—I could sense concern.

"She has some enamel hypoplasia," he finally explained, pointing to the areas of concern. "It's a form of demineralization. But the good news is, we can strengthen her enamel over the next few months."

Relief flooded my chest. Finally, someone was offering a tangible plan.

"Thank you, Dr. David. That gives me hope."

"We'll begin treatments to protect her teeth and prevent further decay," he continued. "And she'll need a spacer to reserve the space for the permanent tooth where the molar was removed. We'll start there. Also, there are early signs of developmental caries on her front teeth. We need to treat those to protect her incoming adult teeth."

But then came a recommendation that made my heart drop—Amariah would need anesthesia for the procedure.

My chest tightened. She was only four, just five months shy of her fifth birthday. My mind immediately flashed back to a haunting dream I'd had months earlier, one in which Amariah didn't survive a medical emergency. That fear gripped me now, body and soul.

"Dr. David, I'm really nervous about this," I said, my voice trembling. "I had a dream a few months ago… and in it, she didn't make it through."

He paused, meeting my eyes with deep empathy. "I truly understand. Your fear is completely valid. But please know—we will take every precaution. We'll do everything possible to keep her safe."

Still, the worry churned inside me.

"I just can't shake it," I admitted, my eyes welling with tears. "What if something goes wrong?"

One of the nurses stepped forward, her voice soft and sincere. "We'll be with her every step of the way. You're not alone. Our team is experienced, and her safety is our top priority."

I nodded slowly, trying to absorb their reassurance.

"I appreciate that. I really do. It's just hard not to worry."

Dr. David gently placed a hand on my shoulder.

"You're a wonderful mother," he said quietly. "Your love for Amariah is so clear. We will take good care of her. I promise."

Later that night, as we prepared for bed, Amariah cuddled beside me, her small body warm against mine. Her eyes held a mix of excitement and nervousness, catching the soft glow of the bedside lamp.

"Mommy, you know what?" she began, her voice a gentle whisper in the quiet room. "Dr. David is really cool. He's not like the other dentists I've had."

"Oh? What makes him so special?" I asked, smoothing her hair and looking into her eyes, eager to understand what had made her feel so at ease.

"He's just… cool," she said, a small smile tugging at her lips. "He talks to me like I'm a big kid. And he made me feel better about the surgery. I'm not as nervous this time."

Her words eased the tension that had been pressing on me all day. As she settled closer, she added, "I'm still a little nervous and a little scared."

I pulled her close, feeling the faint tremble in her voice. "It's okay to be nervous, sweetheart. And it's okay to be scared. It just means you care—and that you're human. You've been through so much with your teeth. I'm so sorry, baby. But I believe Dr. David is going to take really good care of you. Everything's going to be alright."

Later, as I knelt beside her and Michaela, their tiny hands tucked in mine, we said our nightly prayers.

"God, please watch over Amariah during her surgery," I prayed aloud, my voice steady despite the weight of fear within. "We're believing in Your divine intervention and protection."

After tucking them into bed, I returned to my room, my spirit heavy. I sank to my knees, my hands clasped tightly in prayer, and began to speak from the depths of my heart.

"Lord, I'm so scared for Amariah," I cried, tears streaming down my cheeks. "She's only four years old, and the thought of her going under anesthesia terrifies me. I keep dreaming that something will go wrong."

The memory of that haunting dream, where she had died, returned in vivid detail.

"I can't lose her," I sobbed, my voice cracking. "I can't go through that kind of pain. Remember how hard that pregnancy was? The hyperemesis, the Vitamin D deficiency, the homelessness—it was too much. And now, I'm doing this alone, with so much on my shoulders. It's overwhelming."

In the silence that followed, I felt God speak to my heart, reminding me of the rest of that dream—the part where I had brought Amariah to Him, and He had given me the strength to pray her back to life.

"Have faith," He whispered. "Trust in My promises."

Yet the burden in my heart didn't stop with Amariah. My father's stage 4 prostate cancer loomed over me like a dark cloud.

"God, my dad is fighting for his life," I cried out. "Watching him go through this is heartbreaking. How much more can we take? Please, give him strength. Bring healing."

A calm settled over me as I wiped away the tears. In that moment, I knew—despite my fears—I had to trust in God's plan. I had to lean into faith and let it guide me through the uncertainty. I stood, steadied by that divine whisper of hope.

Just before Amariah's surgery, I spoke with my dad. His illness had progressed so far that every conversation felt fragile, urgent. I gathered my courage and asked him how he felt about the possibility of death.

"It's not death that I fear," he said, his voice calm and certain.

He wasn't afraid because he knew exactly where he was going. There was no hesitation, no doubt—only peace.

His faith was steady, and in that moment, I realized he wasn't just enduring illness. He was preparing for something greater. Something eternal.

D-Day: Surgery

As the day arrived, I prayed with all I had, asking God to surround my daughter with protection and peace. That morning, I held Amariah close. Her tiny hand clutched mine.

"Mommy, I'm scared," she whispered, her big eyes looking up at me, wide with fear but full of trust.

"I know, sweetheart," I said, my voice catching. "But Dr. David and the nurses are going to take such good care of you. And I'll be right here, waiting for you."

She nodded bravely, trying to hold back tears.

"Okay, Mommy. I trust you."

Watching her being wheeled into the operating room nearly broke me. My feet felt glued to the floor. If I moved, I might fall apart. My heart beat wildly, and a crushing helplessness settled over me. When the doors closed behind her, I collapsed into a chair, my hands clenched tightly in prayer.

Time slowed. Every second dragged on like hours. Prayer was all I had. It became my breath, my anchor. My father's words echoed: *Hold on to God's unchanging hand.* So I did.

Then, finally, the doors opened. My breath caught. The nurse wheeled her out.

She was groggy, her eyelids fluttering from the anesthesia—but she was breathing. She was alive.

"How is she?" I asked, rushing forward, trying to steady my voice.

"She did great," the nurse said with a warm smile. "It'll take a little time, but she's going to be just fine."

Relief poured over me. A breath I didn't even realize I'd been holding escaped in a soft sob.

"Thank you," I whispered, holding back the flood of tears. "Thank you so much."

I reached for Amariah's hand. It was warm. Solid. Real. And in that moment, the heaviness I had carried began to lift. She had made it through. She was okay.

Later, we picked up her favorite meal from Chick-fil-A and made the quiet drive from Virginia Beach to Norfolk. The silence was thick, broken only by the soft crinkle of the bag beside her.

Usually, she had a bird's appetite, picking at her food gently. But that evening, she barely touched it.

"I'm so tired, Mommy," she murmured, her voice barely audible.

My heart squeezed at her exhaustion. I glanced in the rearview mirror and saw her slumped against the seat, her head resting heavily, her little frame looking even smaller than usual.

So delicate. Yet so strong.

"I know, sweetie," I said gently, offering a smile. "Just rest. We're almost home."

Chapter 7

An Unexpected Journey:
A Glimpse Beyond

*"I know a man in Christ who...
was caught up to the third heaven."*
— 2 Corinthians 12:2-4

Some experiences transcend human understanding. What I saw, what I felt—it was something beyond this world. My journey, too, opened a door to something extraordinary, something sacred, something divine.

Getting Amariah home from the dentist was a feat in itself. Her body, softened and slack with anesthesia, slumped against me like a sleepy doll. I held her close, one arm under her knees, the other bracing her back, as I carried her up the porch steps.

Most of her siblings weren't home—school still held a few in final classes, while the older two had already clocked in at their jobs. The silence in the house felt strange, unsettling. No one bouncing down the stairs two at a time. No soundtrack of chatter and clatter. Just door hinges creaking and floorboards groaning beneath my slow, careful steps.

Inside, the house swallowed the noise of the world and replaced it with stillness.

I carried her into my room and gently laid her in my bed. Her tiny frame folded softly into the blankets like a petal curling inward for the night. Her curls splayed across the pillow. Her fingers rested beside her face, twitchless. I knelt beside her and watched—breath, pause, breath again. Whispered prayers circled silently in my chest, each one a thank-you I couldn't quite speak aloud.

The house remained unnaturally quiet.

Eventually, school let out. The front door eased open and shut again. Backpacks landed near the couch. Microwave buttons chirped. The hush broke.

Soon enough, Michaela peeked into my room, her brow furrowed beneath a sea of curls.

"Mom," she whispered, "is Amariah still alive?"

I turned to her, heart aching at the fear in her tiny voice.
"She's okay, sweetheart. She's still under the sleepy medicine. It'll wear off soon."

But she didn't look convinced.

Then came Richon—my youngest son, pulling at his sleeve like something crawled just beneath his skin. He stood frozen in the doorway before tiptoeing to the edge of the bed.

"She ain't even moved," he whispered.

"She's breathing," I said, gently pointing to her chest. "See that? Like a wave. Up and down."

RJ arrived next, arms folded, concern drawn tight across his face.
"It's been a long time, though," he said. "Longer than when I had surgery."

"Your sister's little," I reminded him. "She's resting deep. But I promise—her body knows what to do."

They nodded reluctantly, and one by one, they drifted back to their routines, carrying their worry like a whisper between them. The hallway hushed again.

The light outside dimmed into soft streaks of lavender and gold. In my room, the quiet stretched.

Then—just shy of 8 p.m.—a flutter.

A twitch of her fingers. A faint movement beneath the covers. Then, slowly, her eyelids lifted, blinking away sleep.

"Come on, little buddy," I whispered.

She blinked up at me, lashes damp at the corners, brows furrowed like she was deciding whether she was home or somewhere else entirely. Her lips parted slightly. Her voice rasped out,
"Mommy… my stomach's saying I'm hungry."

I exhaled a laugh, a bright burst of air wrapped in relief.
"That's my little buddy."

I kissed her forehead, smoothing back her curls.
"I got your favorites, just in case."

I hurried to the fridge and pulled out the Chick-fil-A bag I'd been saving. I slid the nuggets, mac and cheese, and fries onto a plate and warmed them in the microwave while she waited. Her little body was still readjusting—slow, tender, unsure. When I brought her the fruit cup and lemonade first, her whole face lit up.

"Strawberries!" she gasped, clutching the cup like treasure.

"And blueberries too," I said, smiling. "Rainbow snacks for my little buddy."

She pushed herself up with effort, and I tucked another pillow behind her. She settled in and began to eat—slowly, carefully—

each bite deliberate, like she was re-learning the weight of being present in her body. I just watched. I didn't ask questions. I didn't press her.

And then, halfway through her meal, she stopped. One hand hovered in the air, holding a fry.

"Mommy…" she said quietly.

I turned to her fully.
"What's up, little buddy?"

"I gotta tell you something."

Her voice had changed—low and serious, like something ancient had touched her soft frame. She set her food on the tray beside her.

"When I was sleepin'… when I was at the dentist… I went to see Jesus," she said slowly, choosing each word like she was pulling it from a box of treasure she wasn't sure she was supposed to open.

I froze.

"In Heaven," she added with certainty. "He took me there just for a little bit."

I sat on the edge of the bed, not speaking. Just listening. She looked at me with steady eyes—eyes too full of light to belong to a child who had only been four years in this world.

"There were rainbows everywhere, Mommy. Like, everywhere." She spread her arms wide. "And sparkles in the sky. And the grass? It was so soft. Like a blankie."

Tears slid down my cheeks before I could stop them.

She didn't seem to notice. Or maybe she did. But she smiled softly, like she was glad I believed her.

"It was so beautiful," she whispered. "And Jesus held my hand."

The lights from the hallway slipped across the room, pooling at the foot of the bed. But inside this space, it felt like Heaven had cracked open and breathed on us both.

In her tiny voice, in the weight of her little hand clutching mine again, in the glint behind her lashes—

It felt like déjà vu.

Like I'd seen that light before.

Like some part of her had always belonged there... and had simply come back home.

Amariah's eyes shimmered like glass catching morning light. As she sat propped up against the pillows, her little hands clutching her fruit cup, her voice danced with excitement. For the next 45 minutes, she spoke with a joy so pure, so electric, it pulsed through the room.

"Mommy!" she exclaimed, nearly bouncing. "I left my body! I was floating way up high over the dentist's table like a balloon!"

Her eyes widened, and she raised her arms to demonstrate.

"I could see myself lying down. Then guess what? Jesus came—for me! He grabbed my hand and said, 'Wanna fly with me, little buddy?'"

My throat tightened. I reached for her hand, steadying myself in her wonder.

"We zoomed up like whoosh!" she giggled, whipping her hand through the air. "And while we were flying, I got rainbow wings! They were glowing and sparkly, like—like when the sun hits the soap bubbles and makes all the colors." She paused, caught in the memory. "They were so pretty, Mommy. I could fly all by myself!"

"You had wings?" I asked, smiling through misty eyes. "Did you feel like a big butterfly?"

She nodded quickly, curls bouncing. "Yes! A butterfly, and a bird, and a fairy all together! I flapped so high, and Jesus was flying with me. He laughed and spun in the sky, and I copied Him!"

"And did you ask Him to keep those wings?" I prompted gently.

"Uh huh! I said, 'Can I pleeease keep them, Jesus? They're my favorite colors.'" She leaned in close and whispered, "He said I could keep them... but just for a little while."

My heart cracked open at her honesty—childlike, trusting, heavenly.

"What did Jesus look like, baby?" I asked, brushing a crumb from her cheek.

She tilted her head, eyes clouding with thought. "He wore a glowy white robe. It looked warm and floaty. His hair was kinda curly, like reddish-brown. And his face… Mommy, he kinda looked like Stephen Curry. I'm not joking!" She giggled, then added, "His eyes were sparkly—greenish-blue with some brown. Like light was dancing in them. And there was fire. But not ouch fire—heart fire."

I let out a breath I hadn't realized I was holding. "That's so beautiful, Amariah."

She smiled proudly. "He's sooo nice. He called me buddy."

My eyes welled again.

"We flew all the way over the clouds," she continued, "and I could see the city, the big bridges, the shiny water! We went over Virginia Beach, and I saw people walking on sidewalks and holding hands. It looked like ants playing."

Then her voice dropped to a whisper. "I saw Daddy at work. He had on his white lab coat, but guess what? He was still wearing that old hoodie under it! His favorite one."

"And you, Mommy… you were in the waiting room. You had your eyes closed so tight, and you were crying. You kept saying, 'Please God, bring her back. Please don't take my baby.'" Her voice caught. "I saw it all. I heard you."

I covered my mouth, tears slipping freely now.

"Oh, Amariah… I was crying. I was so scared."

"It's okay," she said, her tone surprisingly calm. "Jesus told me you needed me."

"We flew around again and again," she continued. "I saw Brother Richon at school. And RJ and Mael were working. Michaela was at school, doing her paper, I think. And the ocean, Mommy—it was huge! With little fish that sparkled in the sun. And clouds that looked like cotton candy."

She paused to sip her lemonade, then added with glee, "And then I got hungry! Like, really hungry. And I saw Taco John's!"

I blinked. "Wait… you're telling me Jesus took you to Taco John's?"

She nodded eagerly. "Yep! I asked Him if we could stop and eat, and He said, 'Of course we can, buddy!'"

I laughed through my tears. "Jesus ate tacos with you?"

"Mmm-hmm," she said seriously. "We sat in a booth and shared. He even tried the lemonade. He liked it a lot."

Her voice softened to something near reverence.

"Then He took me to my mansion. Mommy—it was huge! Pink and purple with windows everywhere. And no locks! Cuz nobody steals and nobody's scared. Everyone loves everybody."

"What was it like inside?" I asked, leaning in.

"Ohhh Mommy, it was my dream house! Gold floors with sparkly pink dust, like Tinker Bell magic. And all my toys were already there—ALL my favorites. It was bigger than three family homes! Like the ones we saw on the house show."

"Three whole homes? That's a mansion for sure," I whispered.

"Yeah, and I played with Jesus in it. We laughed and He tickled me and chased me around. He said I could stay as long as I wanted. So I said, 'I wanna stay forever.'"

A quiet pause settled over her. Her face changed.

"But He knelt down and said, 'Your mommy needs you. I have to answer her prayers.' I didn't wanna leave, Mommy. I told Him, 'Please, just let me stay.' But He said, 'Not yet. Your time isn't done.'"

She looked down at her lap, fingers curling tightly into her blanket.

"I cried, and He held me real tight and wiped my face. He said I'd lose my rainbow wings when I came back to Earth… but I could get them again when I finished my purpose."

I pulled her close, cradling her like I'd nearly lost her all over again. "I'm so glad you're here, little buddy."

She looked up at me with searching eyes. "But Mommy… why were you so sad? Heaven is so beautiful. It felt like home."

"I know, baby," I said, brushing a tear from her cheek. "But to be in Heaven, you have to leave Earth. And I didn't want to lose you. Not yet. Not ever, if I had it my way."

She rested her head on my shoulder and whispered, "I don't wanna make you sad, Mommy. But I really liked it there."

"I understand," I whispered.

"We played one more time," she said, voice fading. "Then Jesus said it was time. He hugged me again, real tight, and said He'd save my rainbow wings in my mansion. And when I come back again—for good—they'll be waiting."

Tears clung to my lashes.

"When I woke up, I saw Dr. David and the nurses, but I couldn't see you right away. I knew you were in the parent room waiting. I came back for you, Mommy."

She paused, reaching for my hand. "Jesus said I had to."

That night, even as she finally drifted off to sleep around eleven, belly full and cheeks still flushed from telling her story, I couldn't rest. My mind circled back to her words, her wonder, and my own desperate prayer—how Heaven cracked open for a moment and handed me back my daughter.

I sat on the floor beside her bed and pulled out my journal. The house was hushed except for the ticking clock and Amariah's soft, even breaths. By lamplight, I began to write, not wanting to lose a single detail.

Her rainbow wings. Her mansion. Her tacos.

My tears.

I thought back to a vivid dream I'd once had—Amariah lying still in a white box, only to rise again in a place of light. A dream I hadn't dared speak aloud. And now, sitting here, it all came together in a sudden rush:

The dream wasn't just a warning.

It was prophecy.

It was a promise.

A divine echo.

And through my daughter's journey, that promise had touched down on Earth.

So I wrote through the tears, each word an offering. And when I was done, I slipped into bed beside her, pressing my forehead to hers.

"Thank You," I whispered into the dark, over and over again.

Sleep finally found me—cradled in the peace of answered prayer, wrapped in the faint shimmer of rainbow wings.

Chapter 8

Trusting the Journey:
Why I Believe in My Daughter's Heavenly Experience

"Trust in the Lord with all your heart and lean not on your own understanding."
– Proverbs 3:5-6

I wanted answers, explanations, proof. But faith is rarely built on evidence—it's built on trust. My daughter's experience was real, not because I could justify it, but because I knew God had revealed something beautiful beyond comprehension.

A Legacy of Visions

From an early age, I experienced the supernatural. When I shared these moments with my parents, they listened with open hearts. They never made me feel like I was imagining things. Their acceptance was a rare gift. But I soon learned that others weren't so kind. Dismissed, isolated—even called "crazy"—I began to suppress my experiences, confiding only in my parents now and then.

Our family was deeply rooted in the supernatural. My father had a remarkable gift of insight. He often saw visions and had vivid dreams. A devoted student of the Bible, he spent hours reading and dissecting its teachings, effortlessly breaking them down for others. One of his most hauntingly accurate visions came years before 2001: he saw the twin towers fall. When he first shared it, few took notice. But I listened closely. And when 9/11 unfolded, we revisited that vision together. He was stunned that I had remembered. He thought no one had truly heard him.

My mother's prophetic gift ran deep. Looking back, I now understand it was both a blessing and a burden. It shaped the emotional battles she faced while raising us. That realization helped me forgive her strictness. She carried more than the weight of motherhood—she carried visions that often came true with painful accuracy.

She, her sisters, and my grandmother often foresaw deaths, births, pregnancies, and other life-altering events before they happened. Their warnings were rarely wrong. Funerals became a familiar part of my childhood—each one echoing a vision foretold. By the time my father's mother passed—just two weeks before my twelfth birthday—I had stopped keeping count.

A Period of Profound Loss

When my mother pulled me out of performing arts school and enrolled me in our neighborhood high school, it triggered a deep depression. I couldn't express myself anymore. I often felt like the walking dead. I didn't talk about it—I was sure no one would care about the struggles of a teenage girl. I felt invisible. No friends. No real conversations. The only ones who acknowledged me were my teachers. At lunch, I sat alone—until the loneliness became unbearable. Eventually, I stopped going to the lunchroom altogether.

My weight dropped from 140 to 115 pounds. I had constant headaches and nausea. I just didn't feel like eating.

At home, my parents were fighting their own battles. My father had lost his job. Tensions over money turned into daily arguments. As if that weren't enough, both of my grandfathers were terminally ill. Their slow decline cast a long, painful shadow over our family.

I had always been a good student. Books and school were my refuge. But my silence made me invisible. No one noticed the weight loss. No one saw how irritable I'd become—or how deeply sadness had wrapped itself around my spirit.

Grief was coming from every direction—our constant moves, the stress of adjusting to a new school, the emotional breakdown happening inside our home. And then, there was my paternal grandfather.

We shared the same birthday. We had always been close. Watching cancer consume him felt like losing a part of myself. I hadn't even fully processed my grandmother's death four years earlier, and now, another great loss was looming.

Dark thoughts crept in.

I sometimes wondered if escaping the pain altogether was the only way out. At night, I would lie awake, thinking, *If God were merciful, He'd help me leave this earth*. Maybe a sickness would take me. Maybe something would happen—anything to make the pain stop.

But even in that darkness, a small sliver of hope flickered.

I kept reading. I kept praying. Somewhere deep inside, I held on to the belief that my story wasn't meant to end that way.

I didn't yet know what lay ahead. But I would soon discover that even in the most desolate seasons, healing and strength were waiting.

When the Body Fails

After a few weeks at my new school, I came home one afternoon feeling unusually drained. I collapsed on my bed—too tired to eat, study, or speak. At first, my mother told me to rest. She didn't realize something deeper was setting in.

Then the chills hit. Fierce. Unrelenting.

I had felt fine earlier that day, but now, it was like my body was unraveling from the inside out.

When my father got home, he found me trembling, sweating, sneezing, and coughing. Alarmed, he asked if anyone had taken my temperature. No one had. One touch to my forehead was all it took—he knew something was wrong.

He rushed to get a thermometer and children's aspirin. My fever had climbed past 103 degrees—and it was still rising.

Panic set in.

My mother stood frozen, repeating, "We don't have money to take her to the doctor."

My father nodded grimly. "But we have to do something."

My siblings peeked in from the hallway, wide-eyed with worry. The room around me blurred in slow motion.

My dad cracked open the window to let the cool autumn air in. I was burning up, yet still shaking from the cold. As he steadied me to check my temperature again, he handed me aspirin and water, then sat beside me and prayed.

That's the last thing I remember—his whispered words, a tender prayer—before sleep took me for nearly 24 hours.

A Glimpse Beyond

During those 24 hours of sleep, my spirit left my body. I watched from above as my parents joined hands in prayer, gathering my younger siblings close. When they asked if I was dying, my parents didn't answer—they just kept praying.

Then I saw Him. Jesus stood beside me, holding my hand.

He told me my rising fever had brought me dangerously close to death. But instead of fear, He offered to take me on a journey—a glimpse of what could be if I gave up on life.

Scene by scene, I watched my funeral unfold. My body lay peacefully in a white dress I owned, inside a white casket. The sanctuary of Russell Grove Baptist Church in Somerville, Tennessee, overflowed with mourners. I saw my family—my parents, siblings, aunts, and even my grandfather, W.B. Hopson—grieving deeply.

The pain, the sorrow, the blame—it played out before my eyes. My father's heartbreak. The guilt that hung over my family. The arguments, the anger. It was overwhelming.

I turned to Jesus with tears. "Is this what death looks like for me?"

He nodded. "Yes—unless you repent for wanting to die. It's not your time. You still have life—and life more abundantly."

Humbled, I admitted my sadness, my loneliness, my silent wish for escape. I told Him how school, my family, and the weight of rejection had left me empty.

"You are not alone," He said. "I will take care of everything that concerns you. But now, I must answer your father's prayers."

He showed me my dad, sitting quietly at my bedside, praying for healing because he couldn't afford medical care. The love in that moment was tangible.

I didn't want to leave Jesus. There was no pain in His presence—only peace, joy, and a love deeper than anything I'd ever known. But deep in my spirit, I understood: it wasn't time.

With a final embrace, Jesus sent me back—on a cloud of love and restoration.

Back to Life

When I opened my eyes, my father was beside me, silently rejoicing. My mother, tears running down her face, cried out, "Thank you, Jesus!" My younger siblings gathered excitedly around me.

"How do you feel?" my dad asked.

"I'm okay… just hungry."

"You should be. You've been asleep for almost 24 hours."

As I processed what had happened, I shared what I had seen. "I was with Jesus," I said softly. "I saw my funeral. Y'all were all crying. Granddaddy W.B. was there."

They stared in disbelief, unsure what to say. But I had one clear thought: *I need sour cream chips and a Sprite.*

As soon as I told my dad, he didn't hesitate—he grabbed his keys and rushed out to get them. Before he left, he and my mom gave God all the glory, thanking Jesus for answering their prayers and bringing me back.

My mom couldn't stop praising Him. Her voice echoed through the house as she called family and friends, tears of gratitude streaming down her face. "She's awake! She's okay! God did it!"

While she spread the good news, my siblings came into my room, their eyes wide with wonder and relief. They asked where I had been and how I was feeling.

I smiled at them gently. "I was with Jesus," I said. "I saw all of you at my funeral. But He brought me back."

Their eyes grew even wider. I could feel the awe, the curiosity, the emotion rising in the room.

Then I added, "I'm sorry if I've been short with you lately. I wasn't feeling well before. I know I've been distant. But I feel better now. Really, I do."

In that moment, everything in our home shifted—grief turned into gratitude, and fear gave way to faith.

About 30 minutes later, my dad walked in smiling, holding a bag of sour cream chips and a Sprite. He checked my temperature—97.1 degrees. Normal. He gave me aspirin and a cold glass of water. That water tasted like life itself—cool, crisp, and full of grace.

Though still a little dizzy, I got out of bed and took my first steps toward healing.

A New Beginning

Jesus hadn't just brought me back. He had renewed me—spiritually, mentally, emotionally, and physically.

A few days later, I returned to school with a courage I hadn't felt in months. In the lunchroom, I walked over to a group of girls from my English class and asked to sit with them. They welcomed me in. From that day forward, I never ate alone again.

That experience with Jesus forever changed how I saw myself. He had shown me that my life was a gift—that it mattered. Not only was I loved by my family… I was loved by Him.

Chapter 9

Reflections of a Heavenly Journey

"My Father's house has many rooms; if that were not so, would I have told you that I am going there to prepare a place for you?"
– John 14:2

We long to know what lies beyond this life, and Jesus himself gave us a glimpse. I hold onto this promise—what my daughter saw was not a dream, not a fantasy, but a glimpse of the eternal home waiting for all of us.

There's Power in a Name!

As soon as I discovered I was pregnant, I had a strong intuition I was having a girl. I began searching for names. I had planned to name her **Moriah**. The name held deep meaning for me. I was always drawn to the story of Abraham and how he took his son up Mount Moriah in an ultimate act of obedience and faith. It's the place where Abraham was prepared to sacrifice his son of promise, Isaac.

Moriah means "the land of teaching, the land of the Torah, and the land of Yahweh." To me, it symbolized unwavering faith and greatness.

I was also a fan of singer Mariah Carey. Although her name was spelled differently, I associated Moriah with success and strength. I wanted my daughter to embody that same greatness.

One evening, I sat down with my estranged husband and his family to share my decision. "I've decided to name our daughter Moriah," I announced, my voice filled with hope.

Their reactions were immediate and disheartening.

"Moriah? That name has a negative connotation for us," his sister said, frowning. "Remember the neighbor's child? That Moriah was so problematic."

I was taken aback. "What does that have to do with us?" I asked, confused and frustrated. "The name Moriah is biblical—and beautiful."

But their discouragement continued.

"We just can't get past the association," my husband added, shaking his head.

Disheartened, I decided not to use the name. Instead, I turned to the one source that had never let me down—God.

That night, I knelt by my bedside, my heart heavy. "Lord, what should I name my daughter?" I prayed, tears welling in my eyes. "Please guide me and give me a name that will honor You and be a blessing to her."

As I waited in silence, a peace washed over me. I made the decision to keep the name God gave me a secret until her birth. Trusting in His wisdom, I waited.

Each morning before logging into my online college courses, I spent quiet time with God, asking for His guidance. One morning, as I sought clarity on what to name my baby, I felt the Holy Spirit guide me to **2 Chronicles 20**.

Familiar with the story of the Moabites, Ammonites, and Meunites waging war against Jehoshaphat and the Israelites, I flipped back to **Chapter 19**, hoping for deeper insight.

As I read, a name caught my eye—beautiful and unique:

"Amariah the chief priest will be over you in any matter concerning the Lord..." (2 Chronicles 19:11)

The name **Amariah** leapt off the page, glowing in my spirit. Intrigued, I looked up its meaning. Amariah, originally a masculine name in ancient Israel and Judah, had evolved into a feminine name over time. It was most often carried by priests and meant **"Promised by God"** or **"God has said."**

Then I heard a still, calm voice in my spirit: *"This is the name I have approved for you to name your daughter. Do not mention her name to anyone until she is born."*

In that moment, I was overwhelmed. Tears streamed down my face as peace settled over me like a warm blanket. It was the peace Philippians 4:7 describes—*"which surpasses all understanding."*

I've always believed that there is power in a name. And hearing God confirm my daughter's name brought deep reassurance. I knew beyond any doubt that **Amariah** was the name chosen by God. It wasn't just a name—it was a declaration of purpose and promise.

I kept hearing the words from 1 Corinthians 2:9:
"Eyes have not seen, nor ears heard, neither has it entered into the heart of man, the things which God has prepared for those who love Him."

Amariah, my spirit whispered, was destined for a life illuminated by God's love and favor.

Thankfully, my husband and his family stopped asking about the baby's name, allowing me to keep it a complete secret. Because of our separation, he rarely contacted me or the kids. My sister, with whom I lived, was outraged.

"How can he go weeks without talking to his children—let alone his pregnant wife?" she would say, shaking her head.

"I don't understand it either," I'd admit, resigned. "But I've dealt with his selfishness for a long time. The difference now is that everyone else can see it too."

One evening as we sat in the living room, she looked at me with disbelief.

"I just can't respect a man who behaves like that. It's like he's forgotten he's a father."

I sighed. "It's hard. But I'm trying to focus on the positive. God has a plan for us. I believe everything will work out in time."

Through it all, the promise of God's love—and the special name He chose—gave me strength. Knowing that **Amariah** was divinely named kept me grounded in hope, even in the hardest moments. When doubt crept in, I returned to that name. It was more than just a name—it was a promise I could hold in my hands.

Chosen for a Heavenly Experience

At the beginning of 2012, our senior pastor, Pastor Nat, called for a fast. Standing before the congregation, his voice resonated with conviction. "I feel led by the Lord," he began, "for us to participate in a corporate Daniel Fast for 21 days, just as Daniel did in Daniel 6. We need to loosen the bands of wickedness and find resolve for the many challenges we've faced this past year. Participating in this fast will bring us unprecedented breakthroughs."

Though I had fasted intermittently since I was 17, I had never undertaken a 21-day fast. The past seven years had been incredibly tough—a toxic marriage, countless appearances in Juvenile and Domestic Relations Court, struggling to finish my college degree, homelessness, and a high-risk pregnancy. But now, with my baby girl six months old and my body recovering well, I felt ready to take on the challenge. A strong unction from God urged me to follow through with the fast. "There's absolutely nothing to lose," I thought to myself, "but everything to gain from this unique spiritual experience."

As the days of the fast went by, I began to experience vivid visions and dreams about the future. God even reminded me of the visions and dreams I had before my daughter was born, foretelling who she was meant to be. The moment Amariah came into this world, a flood of those visions and dreams cascaded through my mind, each one more striking and vivid than the last. The visions were like snapshots, while the dreams were ethereal and majestic, painting entire landscapes of the future in my sleep.

Some of these dreams centered around Amariah's life—her journey brimming with joy and purpose. Others wove intricate tapestries of her siblings and other family members, their paths intertwined with hers in a dance of love and challenge. Yet, a few dreams carried a foreboding weight, shadows lurking at the edges of my consciousness.

In the quiet hours of the night, I would find myself adrift in these supernatural experiences, unsure of whom to confide in. My mind would wander to my parents, who always seemed to have a way of understanding the unspoken and offering guidance when I felt lost.

One evening, as I sat by the dim glow of a bedside lamp, I whispered softly in prayer, "I've been having these dreams," my voice trembling with uncertainty. "They're so vivid, so real… I don't know what to make of them. Help me to understand them."

As I meditated on these recent supernatural experiences, a profound sense of purpose settled within me. I felt strongly that these visions and dreams were not mere random occurrences—they were divine gifts, meant to be heeded. There was something very special and profound that Amariah brought with her from the moment of her birth.

With newfound resolve, I decided I would journal my experiences, capturing every detail and emotion, and I would pray for guidance. With each entry, I found solace and clarity. The pages of my journal became a testament to the extraordinary journey that lay ahead for Amariah, her siblings, and me.

A week after our fast ended, Valentine's Day approached. I was sitting in church, cradling Amariah in my arms while my oldest daughter and youngest son were in the kid's church. Amariah was singing joyfully, her sweet voice filling the room as the service ended. Just as I was preparing to gather my things and pick up my other children, a woman with a radiant smile approached me. She wore a beautiful golden dress and shiny patent leather black pumps. I had seen her before in passing, but we had never really spoken.

"Hi there," she said warmly, adjusting her red and gold glasses. "I'm Sister Janice, and you are?"

"I'm Tappe," I replied.

"Good to meet you, Tappe," she said with great enthusiasm. "Is this your baby?"

"Yes," I answered with a smile. "She's my youngest. She's six months old."

Amariah, nibbling on her left hand, looked at Janice with wide eyes and began to smile and laugh as Sister Janice spoke to her.

"My, aren't you a happy and joyful baby," Janice cooed. "Is she like this all the time?"

"Yes," I replied happily. "She is always happy, laid-back, and easygoing. She is a joy to have around. I'm very grateful, especially after having such a rough and high-risk pregnancy."

"God knows how to do it! I'm glad He gave you beauty for ashes," Janice said, her voice filled with warmth.

I nodded in agreement. "Yes, ma'am."

"Well, I came over to tell you something that I saw. I'm a seer. Do you know what that is? Have you ever heard of that?" she inquired.

"Yes, I have. I come from a legacy of seers—my mom, my dad, my grandmothers on both sides, my aunts on my mother's side. So yes, ma'am. I'm very familiar with the term 'seer.'"

"Good," she replied, relieved. "I didn't want to spook you or anything. I just wanted to tell you that God wanted me to let you know that your labor is not in vain. He showed you some things, didn't He, concerning your daughter? Do you believe in prophecy?"

"Yes," I replied. "He showed me that my daughter is going to do something extraordinary. I saw that she was going to have supernatural experiences that would be shared with the world and with those around her. He didn't give me all the sordid details, but He's been giving me these snapshot visions and dreams of her performing before huge crowds."

"Ah ha!" she said with a hearty laugh. "He sent me to confirm to you that what you have seen about your daughter will come to pass. What you have seen about all your children will come to pass. You're a dreamer just like Joseph in the Bible. You have seer abilities just like the Old Testament prophets—Elijah, Jeremiah, Samuel, and more. The reason I'm focused on this one is because you had a very difficult pregnancy with her, with several challenges that were not your fault. There were other people who contributed to those difficulties, and I especially see one person. This person is running from God just like Jonah and is bringing chaos into your life. God wants me to let you know that He knows, He sees, and He is going to deal with those folks for your sake, your daughter's sake, and your other children's sakes. Divine judgment is coming just as the Lord has promised. He said, 'Vengeance is mine, I will repay.' Trust and believe that your Heavenly Father definitely has your back for the many wrongs that have been done to you and your children. He is going to do just as He promised in the book of Matthew 5. He's going to reward you openly for all that you have done in secret. You have been faithful. In the coming days, God is going to reward you openly for all that you have endured and done in secret. It's not that you haven't made mistakes—He's showing me that you have—but He wants you to know that while man looks at the outside, God looks on the inside. God sees the heart.

He sees your heart, and He's got much in store for you, your baby, and the rest of your kids, too. It's going to require some changing and rearranging, but you have sacrificed so many things, and God sees your sacrifice. He's going to come through for you. He's got your back. He sees you."

Tears began to flow like a river from my eyes. Sister Janice reached out to give me a comforting hug.

"Oh, how He loves you, my sister. He has not forgotten you. Go in peace and be encouraged," she whispered softly.

Sister Janice's words pierced my heart deeply. Though she physically hugged me, it felt as though God Himself had embraced me that day. He had sent another seer to tell me that He had seen my pain and heard my tears. He was keeping record of all the wrongs and was going to reward me openly. Tears continued to stream freely. My mind drifted to the story of Hagar and Sarai in Genesis 16.

In Genesis 16:7-13 (NIV), we read:

"The angel of the Lord found Hagar near a spring in the desert; it was the spring that is beside the road to Shur. And he said, 'Hagar, slave of Sarai, where have you come from, and where are you going?' 'I'm running away from my mistress Sarai,' she answered. Then the angel of the Lord told her, 'Go back to your mistress and submit to her.' The angel added, 'I will increase your descendants so much that they will be too numerous to count.' The angel of the Lord also said to her: 'You are now pregnant, and you will give birth to a son. You shall name him Ishmael, for the Lord has heard of your misery. He will be a wild donkey of a man; his hand will be against everyone and everyone's hand against him, and he will live in hostility toward all his brothers.' She gave this name to the Lord who spoke to her: 'You are the God who sees me,' for she said, 'I have now seen the One who sees me.' That is why the well was called Beer Lahai Roi; it is still there, between Kadesh and Bered."

I could relate to Hagar's feelings when she referred to God as *El Roi*, the God who sees. As a servant with virtually no rights and no voice, she felt unseen and unheard. While my situation was different, I understood her sense of invisibility. Her mistress had both marital and societal upper hands. Before that day when Sister Janice spoke those words to me, I too felt a little invisible. However, after hearing those words of confirmation, I had blessed assurance that, like Hagar, I had met the God who sees those who endure situations where they feel unseen, unheard, overlooked, and forgotten.

Chapter 10

Embracing the Next Chapter

"Let us run with perseverance the race marked out for us."
– Hebrews 12:1

The journey doesn't end—it continues, shaping us into who we are meant to be. I will keep going, not because the path is easy, but because I know God is leading me forward, step by step, toward something greater.

One of the greatest things I have learned from my daughter's extraordinary experience is that God hears my prayers. The very fact that she and Jesus spoke about her return from Heaven to Earth because of my prayers is simply amazing—and deeply encouraging. It brings the scripture James 5:16 to life: "The fervent, effectual prayers of the righteous availed much."

Prayer has been the cornerstone of my life for as long as I can remember. From my childhood, whenever I faced a challenge, my first instinct was always to pray. It was woven into every part of my upbringing—at school events, in church, among neighbors, and throughout our daily lives. Prayer wasn't just a practice; it was a constant presence. My parents prayed daily, as did my grandparents and many other family members. Growing up in such a prayer-saturated environment, it became deeply ingrained in me as the ultimate answer to life's struggles and uncertainties.

I remember one quiet evening when Amariah, with her innocent eyes and gentle smile, came to me and said, "Mommy, do you know Jesus told me He had to bring me back to you?"

My heart skipped a beat, and I asked softly, "What did He say to you? Tell me more."

"He said He brought me back because of your prayers," she replied, her voice filled with a childlike certainty that brought tears to my eyes.

"What do you think about that?" I inquired.

"I think it's cool. I wanted to stay there in Heaven in my purple and pink mansion, playing with my toys—but I was happy to go back home too."

It felt as though a divine light had entered our home, illuminating the power and reach of prayer. In that moment, I realized the incredible honor and privilege it is to know that my prayers reached the courts of Heaven and were delivered directly to God the Father. That reassurance pushed me to take an even deeper dive into my prayer life.

My thoughts drifted back to those quiet nights when doubt and fear would creep in. I'd kneel beside my bed and pour my heart out to God. "Lord, I need Your guidance," I'd whisper, the weight of the world pressing on my shoulders. "Show me the way and help me to have unwavering faith."

Knowing my words weren't ignored gave me strength. As I continued to pray fervently, I felt a profound connection to the divine. It was as if my soul were in direct conversation with God—each prayer a testament to my faith and hope.

Every answered prayer, every moment of divine intervention, reaffirmed the truth of James 5:16. Prayer became not just a spiritual practice, but a lifeline. It gave me strength in hard times, courage in uncertainty, and hope when things seemed hopeless.

Amariah told me that before Jesus returned her to me, He gave her a profound and unforgettable message—a message about love. He explained that love was the reason He came from Heaven to Earth. Every act He performed—teaching, healing, delivering—was driven by love. "I died on the cross because of love," He told her gently.

"Everything I do for My children is rooted in love," He said. "I desire what is best for you, even when My love comes in the form of discipline. That tough love is always for your ultimate good. My love for My children is like the love your mother has for you and your siblings—but infinitely greater."

Amariah's eyes sparkled with emotion as she shared His words. "He wants me to spread the message of His love to others," she said with a sense of purpose. "So many people think God hates them, but He doesn't. He really, really loves us, and He wants everyone to come back and live with Him in Heaven."

Her words moved me to tears. The depth of Jesus's love, expressed through Amariah, overwhelmed me. It reminded me that His love is unwavering, boundless, and more powerful than we can imagine—a love that surpasses even the deep love I felt from my earthly father.

"He told me His love is the reason for everything He does," she continued, her voice trembling. "And He wants us to share this message with the world."

In that moment, I felt the weight of her message. It wasn't just sweet—it was sacred. I was reminded of the ultimate sacrifice Jesus made for us, giving His life on the cross purely out of love. He died for one reason and one reason alone: because He loves us.

One of my favorite scriptures came to mind: "We love because he first loved us" (1 John 4:19). That verse captures the essence of everything Jesus taught Amariah. Love is not just a comforting truth—it is a command and a way of life. Love must be our motivation in all things: toward God, toward ourselves, and toward one another.

As I reflect on Amariah's miraculous experience, I am filled with gratitude for the lessons it taught us and the light it brought into our lives. What was meant to be a simple dental procedure became a divine encounter. At just four years old, Amariah journeyed beyond the clouds, into a realm few ever witness, and returned with a message too powerful to ignore. She spoke not as a child, but with clarity and wisdom beyond her years. Her descriptions of Heaven were vivid—full of love, peace, and connection to something greater. It felt as though she had been chosen to glimpse the divine and return to share it with the rest of us.

In many ways, her experience echoed a dream I had long before her surgery—a dream that etched itself onto my heart. I was peacefully driving along a quiet highway when an angelic figure appeared, instructing me to take an unusual left exit. Trusting the divine voice, I turned and found myself in the aftermath of a terrible school bus accident. Panic flooded me as I feared for my daughters, Michaela and Amariah, who were on a field trip.

I found Michaela first—she was helping injured children, calm and strong beyond her age. But Amariah was nowhere to be found. Then came the devastating news from medics: Amariah had passed away. They presented her to me in a beautiful white and gold box. My world shattered. I fell to my knees, desperate and broken, crying out to God for help.

Suddenly, I was transported to a heavenly realm filled with indescribable light and peace. There, in Jesus's presence, I was told to call Amariah back to life, just as Jairus had done for his daughter in scripture. Though trembling with fear, I obeyed. To my amazement, Amariah was restored. Together, we returned to the highway, where people stood in awe. Many came to us, asking for prayer and healing for their hurting children.

Though I awoke from the dream with lingering questions, its meaning became clear over time. One of the greatest lessons it revealed was the power of obedience. In the face of fear and uncertainty, I chose to trust God. That obedience opened the door to a miracle.

I still remember the look on Jesus's face as I obeyed His instruction. His joy was radiant—like a proud parent watching a child take their first steps. His eyes were full of warmth and delight, a glow that wrapped around me like the heartbeat of Heaven itself. In that look, I saw His pleasure, not just in my action, but in my trust. And that trust gave Him space to move powerfully on my behalf.

In that sacred moment, it felt as though my obedience became a key that unlocked the fullness of His promise, setting His divine power into unstoppable motion. The words of scripture came alive with a clarity I had never experienced:

"But Samuel replied, 'Does the Lord delight in burnt offerings and sacrifices as much as in obeying the Lord? To obey is better than sacrifice, and to heed is better than the fat of rams.'"
— 1 Samuel 15:22

Those words weren't just distant wisdom from an ancient text—they surged with life, purpose, and undeniable strength. Obedience wasn't merely an obligation; it became a lifeline, an act of faith that bridged the vast chasm between fear and miracles. I understood, more deeply than ever before, that obedience is not just a choice—it is an invitation for God to manifest His will and wonders in our lives.

Through that experience, my faith in divine healing was immeasurably strengthened. I learned that even when the path seems daunting, surrendering to God's will draws His presence closer. His promises become tangible, His love unmistakable, and His guidance unwavering. Obedience doesn't simply please

Him—it opens the gates to possibilities far beyond human comprehension.

Years later, when Amariah returned to me from her real-life heavenly journey during surgery, it was as though the dream and reality converged. Her words, filled with wisdom and clarity, echoed the divine encounter I had experienced years earlier. Her heavenly adventure affirmed everything I had seen in that dream—the presence of God's love, the power of prayer, divine healing, and the miracle of restoration.

Now, as I watch Amariah grow into a young woman, nearing 14, I see the continuing legacy of that dream and her journey. Her spirit radiates kindness, grace, and an undeniable sense of purpose—one shaped by the divine touch she experienced. Her story has become a transformative touchstone, not just for her, but for everyone who knows her.

Since her divine encounter at just four and a half years old, Amariah's visions and dreams have grown both in frequency and depth. She has seen everything from reconciliations between estranged family members to deeply personal revelations—visions of death and funerals within our family. Among these extraordinary dreams, the one that remains most profound was her vision of my mother's passing.

In February 2023, after my mother suffered a debilitating stroke, Amariah began to describe vivid dreams of her grandmother's death and funeral. Her words were tender but carried a certainty that was impossible to ignore, as if she had seen a moment that had yet to unfold.

One year and nine months later, my family and I faced the heartbreaking reality of laying my mother to rest beside my father and youngest brother. What struck me most was how closely the funeral mirrored Amariah's vision. My mother wore a stunning lavender dress and rested in a matching lavender casket, surrounded by vibrant flowers—just as Amariah had seen. The funeral home in Memphis ensured that every detail carried the regal elegance she had described. It was more than a farewell—it was an affirmation, a sacred echo of what had already been shown through God's grace.

Amariah's gift continues to remind us of the mysterious and miraculous ways God speaks, especially through those with open hearts. For me, as her mother, this journey has been both humbling and illuminating. I've learned to walk by faith and not by sight—to trust in God's plan, even when the road ahead is unclear. Amariah's life and her encounter with Heaven continue to remind me of the miracles surrounding us, waiting patiently to be seen.

Another remarkable thread in our story is God's use of rainbows. Since 2015—a year before my father's passing from cancer—I've come to recognize that God often sends me a rainbow as a divine reminder of His faithfulness. These gentle displays appear in unexpected moments, but they arrive with precision, speaking to promises made and promises kept.

In Genesis 9:12–17, we are given this divine reassurance:

"And God said, 'This is the sign of the covenant I am making between me and you and every living creature with you, a covenant for all generations to come:
I have set my rainbow in the clouds, and it will be the sign of the covenant between me and the earth.
Whenever I bring clouds over the earth and the rainbow appears in the clouds, I will remember my covenant between me and you and all living creatures of every kind. Never again will the waters become a flood to destroy all life.
Whenever the rainbow appears in the clouds, I will see it and remember the everlasting covenant between God and all living creatures of every kind on the earth.'
So God said to Noah, 'This is the sign of the covenant I have established between me and all life on the earth.'"

This passage remains one of the most beautiful and sacred affirmations of God's enduring love. Just as He gave Noah a promise, He continues to speak today—through rainbows, through dreams, through the quiet whispers that meet us in our still moments.

God is faithful. His heart overflows with love for His children, even as they face trials and uncertainty. In His wisdom, He allows us the gift of free will, giving us space to think, choose, and walk our paths. Yet, in His boundless love, He gently nudges us toward deeper faith—calling us to trust beyond logic, to believe beyond sight.

This book is more than a reflection of my daughter's experience—it is a testament to the sustaining power of faith, the transformative reach of love, and the resilience of hope. My prayer is that her story will awaken others to the presence of God in their own lives. That it will encourage you to treasure your loved ones more deeply, to trust the divine guidance whispering through your days, and to believe in the unseen that surrounds you.

Though this chapter of her story concludes, her journey is far from over. *Her Rainbow Wings* will remain a sacred reminder of God's promises—an ever-present sign that something greater always waits just beyond the clouds.

Afterword:
Trusting the Journey

R*ainbow Wings: A Young Girl's Journey to Heaven and Back* is more than a memoir—it is a testament to faith, resilience, and the undeniable presence of God.

Through every trial, every revelation, and every moment of doubt, one truth has remained constant: God's love is unwavering, His promises are real, and His divine hand guides us through even the most uncertain paths.

Writing this book has been a deeply personal experience—one woven with faith, healing, and the understanding that life's challenges are never without purpose. My daughter's journey reminded me that even in the darkest moments, God's presence never left us. There were times when fear threatened to consume me, when exhaustion clouded my vision, and when uncertainty loomed over every decision. But through it all, I was reminded again and again that God sees, He hears, and He answers.

Her experience was not just for her—it was for me, for our family, and perhaps for you, the reader. Her story was never meant to remain only ours. It was meant to be shared, to uplift, and to serve as a reminder that heaven is closer than we think, and that life itself is a gift.

If you've ever questioned your own journey, I encourage you to trust that your life has meaning—even in the most uncertain moments. Trust the process. Trust the lessons. Trust Him.

I pray that, within these pages, you have found something familiar: a reflection of your own journey, a spark of renewed faith, or simply a gentle reassurance that God is with you—always.

May you walk forward with courage. May you embrace your next chapter. And may you always remember that your story matters, your life has purpose, and heaven is watching over you.

Thank you for walking this path with me. May you find hope in your own journey, and may you always recognize the wings that carry you forward.

With love and gratitude,
Tappe Hopson

www.ingramcontent.com/pod-product-compliance
Lightning Source LLC
Chambersburg PA
CBHW070853050426
42453CB00012B/2172